Start an Export Business from the USA

A complete guide from company registration to export step-by-step

Especially for aspiring entrepreneurs, working professionals, students and job seekers

MD SAHID

GLOVYA EXIM

Glovya Exim

Start an Export Business from the USA- A complete guide from company registration to export step-by-step

For permission requests, please get in touch with the author at:
Email: mohammadsahid.star@gmail.com

Disclaimer: The information contained in this book is for general informational purposes only. However, the author assumes no responsibility or liability for any errors, omissions, or changes in applicable laws, regulations, or procedures that may occur after publication. Readers should consult with appropriate professionals for specific advice tailored to their needs.

ISBN-13: **978-93-343-8427-7**
First Edition: **2025**
Self-Published Author: **Md Sahid**
Published by: **Glovya Exim** (The Imprint, Glovya Exim is a registered trademark of Md Sahid)

Contents

Preface

Start an Export Business from the USA- A complete guide from company registration to export step-by-step is essential for entrepreneurs and business owners looking to expand their horizons and venture into the global market. This comprehensive book provides a clear, structured pathway to help you navigate the complexities of exporting from the U.S.

This guide covers all aspects of the export process, from understanding export readiness and conducting thorough market research to obtaining necessary licenses and finding reliable suppliers. Each chapter is meticulously designed to offer practical advice, detailed procedures, and helpful tips, ensuring you are well-equipped to tackle the challenges of international trade.

The book is enriched with numerous helpful website links that provide valuable resources, regulatory information, and support services, whether you're looking to understand customs procedures, secure funding, protect intellectual property, or implement effective marketing strategies.

MD SAHID

Introduction

Why Export from The U.S.

The U.S. exports some $3 trillion in goods and services to world markets annually, there is a vast opportunity to increase both the number of U.S. exporters and the markets they are selling to—particularly among small and medium-sized firms. Here are just a few reasons to pursue export sales:

Demand. More than 95 percent of the world's consumers are outside of the United States. Your competitors are increasing their global market share, and you can too.

Access. Exporting doesn't have to be burdensome. The Internet, improved logistics channels, free trade agreements, e-commerce, and the array of available export assistance through the U.S. government and its partners has made exporting more achievable; that's true for even the smallest businesses.

Profitability. Exporting can be profitable for businesses of all sizes. On average, sales grow faster, more jobs are created, and employees earn more than in non-exporting firms.

Competitive Advantage. The United States is known worldwide for high quality, innovative goods and services, customer service, and sound business practices.

Risk Mitigation. Most companies that export have an easier time riding out fluctuations in the U.S. economy, and are more likely to stay in business.

Export Resources. U.S. companies can benefit from U.S. government resources and its state and local partners. For example, the U.S. Department of Commerce has a global network of U.S.

Commercial Service offices in 100+ U.S. cities and U.S. embassies and consulates in more than 80 international markets. Trade professionals offer export counseling and a range of customized export solutions. They can also put businesses in touch with key resources such as export financing through the U.S. Export-Import Bank and Small Business Administration.

Export Potential by Product in The World Market (Estimate for 2029)

The products with greatest export potential from the United States to World Are Motor vehicles for the transport of <10 persons, Soya beans, and Human & animal blood, blood fractions & immunological products. Soya beans show the largest absolute difference between potential and baseline exports in value terms, leaving room to realize additional exports worth $29 bn, representing 3.8% of unrealized export potential.
https://exportpotential.intracen.org/en/products/tree-map?fromMarker=i&exporter=842&toMarker=w&market=w&whatMarker=k

What Is Exporting

In the day-to-day course of doing business, most U.S. companies producing U.S. goods and services may not be familiar with the different ways the terms "export" and "import" are used in international trade.

Access to U.S. government export promotion assistance, programs, and financing depends on whether the goods or services being sold are produced in the United States. As such, it is important for U.S.

businesses to be familiar with the different, sometimes confusing ways the terms "export" and "import" are used in different contexts.

U.S. Exports/U.S. Exporting/U.S. Exporter: Only U.S. exports are eligible for U.S. government assistance, services, and financing. For goods or services to be considered U.S. exports, they must be created, produced or manufactured in the United States. Depending on the geographic point of reference, U.S. exports may be referred as:

- "U.S. exports TO a foreign market/country" FROM the United States" or
- "Imports FROM the United States TO a foreign market/country."
- "Selling/shipping/delivering U.S. produced goods or services to a buyer in a foreign market.

Product Selection

Questions to Consider

You must consider several issues when you are thinking of selling overseas, including:

- What foreign needs does your product satisfy?
- What products should your company offer abroad?
- Should your company modify its domestic market product for sale abroad? Should it develop a new product for the foreign market?
- What specific features, such as design, color, size, packaging, brand, labels, and warranty, should your product have? How important are languages or cultural differences?
- What specific services, warranties, and spare parts are necessary abroad at the presale and post-sale stages?
- Are your company's service and repair facilities adequate?

Product Adaptation

Selecting the right product for export from the U.S. is a strategic decision that can make or break your business. Here's a structured approach to help you choose wisely:

Key Criteria for Product Selection:

- **Market Demand**: Focus on products with proven demand in your target countries. Use tools like the Export Potential Map to identify high-demand items.

- **Competitive Advantage**: Choose products where the U.S. has a technological, quality, or branding edge—think medical devices, software, or specialty foods.
- **Profit Margins**: Ensure the product offers healthy margins after factoring in production, logistics, tariffs, and marketing costs.
- **Regulatory Compliance**: Check export regulations, certifications, and labeling requirements for each target market.
- **Product Adaptability**: Select items that can be customized for different cultural or functional needs abroad.
- **Sourcing Availability**: Select the product which is easily available in the U.S.
- **Lightweight/Compact**: Cheaper and easier to ship internationally.
- **Legally Exportable**: No special export license or restriction involved.

Products to Avoid (As a Beginner)

- Require export licenses (e.g., military, firearms, tech)
- Spoil quickly or need refrigeration
- Are heavy, bulky, or hazardous
- Are already dominated by large brands unless you offer unique value

Branding, Labeling & Packaging

Consumers are concerned with both the product itself and the product's secondary features, such as packaging, warranties, and services. Branding and labeling products in foreign markets raise new considerations for your company, such as:

- Are international brand names important to promote and distinguish a product? Conversely, should local brands or private labels be used to heighten local interest?
- Are the colors used on labels and packages offensive or attractive to the foreign buyer? For example, in some countries certain colors are associated with death.
- Can labels and instructions be produced in official or customary languages if required by law or practice?
- Does information on product content and country of origin have to be provided?
- Are weights and measures stated in the local unit? Even with consumer products, packaging and describing contents in metric measurements (e.g., kilograms, liters) can be important.
- Must each item be labeled individually? What is the language of the labeling? For example, "Made in the U.S." may not be acceptable; the product may need to be labeled in the language spoken by the country's consumers. There may be special labeling requirements for foods, pharmaceuticals, and other products.
- Are local tastes and knowledge considered? A cereal box with the picture of a U.S. athlete on it may not be as attractive to overseas consumers as the picture of a local sports hero.

Installation

Another element of product preparation that your company should consider is the ease of installing the product overseas. If technicians or engineers are needed overseas to assist in installation, your company should minimize their time in the field if possible. To do so, your company may wish to pre-assemble or pretest the product before shipping or to provide training for local service providers through the web. Your U.S. brand name is important to you, but it may be less important to foreign consumers. On the other hand, in some places, it may be more valuable than it is in the U.S. visible endorsement from a famous person may get you sales at home, but the same person may be unknown—or, worse, disliked—elsewhere.

Your company may consider disassembling the product for shipment and reassembling it abroad. This method can save your company shipping costs, but it may delay payment if the sale is contingent on an assembled product. Your company should be careful to provide all product information, such as training manuals, installation instructions (even relatively simple instructions), and parts lists, in the local language.

International Market Research

International market research is a key piece of successful export planning. It is important to critically review and assess if the potential export destination is suitable for your product or service. You need to determine if there is a market, if your product is competitive after determining the landed cost, and then the most cost-effective and time-efficient export strategy.

Research Process

Start by collecting trade data to gauge market size. Look for where opportunities may exist, whether demand is increasing or decreasing, and if there is competition.

For smaller companies, identifying 3 to 5 potential markets might be a good number to explore. You may also group potential countries by largest markets, fastest growing markets, and smaller markets with high growth.

Then review country and industry reports to assess market conditions, opportunities and challenges. This will help you decide which markets represent the best opportunities and are worth the investment of additional resources.

Step 1: Develop Your Research Questions

If you are a **new exporter**, consider:

- How large are your potential markets?
- What countries/markets are currently buying products like yours?

- Who are your competitors, from which countries do they come, and how large are they?
- What are the required standards, testing, and certifications?
- Do your products (or their labeling or packaging) need to be modified for one or more markets?
- What duties, taxes, and other costs apply? What are the shipping costs and partner margins? What is the landed cost, or total export price?
- Is your price point appealing within the market? If not, what can you do to make it more appealing?
- What distribution channels are available?

If you are an **active exporter** considering a new export market, or re-assessing a current market, it is equally important to conduct this market research as conditions frequently change. For example, there could be different shipping costs, tariffs, and regulations affecting your business. The goal of market research is to learn about:

- The largest markets and/or fastest-growing markets for your product.
- The market trends and outlook for your industry in that country.
- The competitive landscape for your industry/product in that country, and potentially in the region.
- The costs associated with getting your product from your facility to customers in another country, i.e. the landed cost.

- Any required product changes (and associated costs) to comply with the destination country's regulations and standards.

Step 2: Conduct Research

Primary market research is information collected directly from the foreign marketplace through interviews, surveys, and other direct contact with representatives and potential buyers. Attending trade shows (in the U.S. or in international locations), conferences, or other industry venues can be useful places for many primary market research conversations.

The advantage of primary market research is that you tailor it to your company's needs and specific questions. However, it can be time-consuming and expensive — and may not be comprehensive.

Secondary market research is information obtained from other sources, such as trade statistics or reports for a country or a product. This information tends to be less expensive, and in some cases, free.

Sources

Trade Data

To get a complete picture, look at both U.S. export statistics and a foreign country's import statistics for the past few years.

There are a number of resources online to help exporters find and use export and import data. These resources range from U.S. government sites to multinational organizations such as the United Nations, to foreign government sites. Additionally, industry associations may collect and compile trade data and make it available to members.

Many trade data resources use the Harmonized System (Hs) Code to provide details on growth or decline of exports in general, as well as data related to specific products.

Foreign Import Statistics

Find and analyze foreign import statistics by country to see which countries are importing your type(s) of products. Also consider complementary products, especially if your HS code is very general. Foreign import statistics will help you get a better sense of the broad demand for your product(s) than U.S. export statistics typically will.

- Take note of which countries are importing the most of your type of product(s). You can look at overall value and the volume of imports.
- Look for trends to see if the import market is expanding or declining over the last few years.
- Identify smaller markets that are experiencing high growth despite lower import values. They may be emerging markets with less competition.

U.S. Export Statistics

Find and analyze U.S. export statistics by country to see which countries are importing your type of product(s) from the U.S. Again, use complementary products if your HS code is very general. U.S. export statistics can help you to identify markets that are more favorable markets for U.S. companies.

- Compare U.S. export statistics for your product(s) with the foreign import statistics. If the U.S. exports represent a larger percentage of the imports, it might be an indicator that the market has a preference for U.S. products and that market conditions are favorable to U.S. companies. For countries where U.S. exports represent a lower percentage, it could mean that there are market conditions that make it a more challenging market for U.S. companies. That does not necessarily mean it is not a good market for your products, but that additional research is required to look at market conditions.

- U.S export statistics can also help to identify to which markets your domestic competitors are exporting, which can be helpful as you plan your market entry strategies.
- Review U.S. and state export level data, available through **TradeStats Express** to identify the largest export markets, which may reflect the competitive advantages of your state and/or historical trading partners. The data you find may help you also develop a competitive pricing strategy.

Country-Specific Research

For countries, look up data on population size and makeup, per capita income, and production levels by industry. These are important indicators of market potential for your company's products. Resources for this type of information include, among others:

- U.S. Commercial Service **Country Commercial Guides** (CCGs)
- U.S. Commercial Service **Market Intelligence**
- **United Nations Statistical Yearbook**
- **The World Bank Data Catalog**
- CIA **World Factbook**
- **International Monetary Fund (IMF) Data**

Industry-Specific Research

For specific industries, find market information at:

- U.S. Commercial Service **Market Intelligence**
- U.S. Department of Commerce **Top Markets Reports**
- U.S. Department of Agriculture **Foreign Agricultural Service** (FAS)
- U.S. Department of Commerce **Office of Textiles & Apparel** (OTEXA)
- **Alcohol & Tobacco Tax & Trade Bureau** (ATTB)
- U.S. Department of Commerce **National Travel and Tourism Office**

Step 3: Review Potential Markets

For most small businesses, 3-5 foreign markets are enough - initially. You may want to test one market and then move on to secondary markets as your experience level develops. Additionally, it can be more cost-effective to focus on geographic regions rather than markets scattered around the globe.

Using the resources from your primary and secondary market research, evaluate the potential based on your research questions (above) and these additional factors:

- Consistent market growth, and/or industry sector growth in the other country
- Free Trade Agreement with the U.S.
- Specific region within the country to target instead of the whole country
- Demand for your type of product or related products to gauge overall consumption trends

- Presence of local or other international competitors
- Environment for your marketing material (costs of translation, does your product's name translate accurately?)
- Tariff or non-tariff barriers that might affect your product

Step 4: Develop an Export Plan

Once you have decided that your company is able to export and committed to it, develop your export plan with the data and insights you found. A customized export plan is a valuable strategic and operational tool for growing your export business.

You may conclude that your marketing resources would be applied more effectively to a few select countries. Exporting to a manageable number of countries allows you to focus your resources without jeopardizing your existing U.S. sales efforts.

Also, there are other items you should consider when selecting your initial markets.

It takes time to build an international business - often months, and sometimes years, to see a return on investment. By committing to the written plan, you can help ensure that your company continues to work towards long-term goals.

Selecting Initial Export Market

Once you have completed your initial market research, and determined which markets have the best potential for your product or service, it is critical to review the steps needed to actually enter the market.

Regulatory, logistical, and cultural factors can all play a role in market entry. Some questions to consider include:

- Are there any infrastructure/logistical factors which could make my product or service difficult to access for local consumers?
- If there is a language difference, how will you communicate with potential partners and customers?
- Are there any U.S. Export Controls on my product to this destination?
- Are there import requirements that may necessitate an alteration of my product?
- Once the market is entered, how will after-sales service be conducted, or customers' questions addressed?
- How can you mitigate risk in case of shipping issues, non-payment, or other disputes?

Additionally, it's important to work with reputable partners to support your company in the export process, including a logistical provider, Customs Broker, attorney, accountant, and bank. As you create your market entry plan, the advice of these partners can help you save time and money and avoid potential issues.

Finally, a reputable, reliable, and knowledgeable local partner can help make your market entry successful. Your local partner should be familiar with the import requirements, especially Customs clearance requirements for your product, and know the major industry players and/or potential customers. The local representative may also register your product for sale locally, and in some cases may then have rights to the product design/trademark, etc. Make sure you conduct due diligence on a partner and consult with an attorney to design contracts that protect your company.

Free Trade Agreements (FTA)

Selling to U.S. Free Trade Agreement (FTAs) partner countries can help your company to enter and compete more easily in the global marketplace through reduced trade barriers. U.S. FTAs address a variety of foreign government activities that affect your business: reduced tariffs, stronger intellectual property protection, opportunities for U.S. exporter input in the development of FTA partner country product standards, fair treatment for U.S. investors, enhanced opportunities to compete for foreign government procurements, and opportunities for U.S. service companies.

What are Free Trade Agreements?

A Free Trade Agreement (FTA) is an agreement between two or more countries where the countries agree on certain obligations that affect trade in goods and services, and protections for investors and intellectual property rights, among other topics. For the United States, the main goal of trade agreements is to reduce barriers to U.S. exports, protect U.S. interests competing abroad, and enhance the rule of law in the FTA partner country or countries.

Currently, the United States has 14 FTAs with 20 countries. FTAs can help your company to enter and compete more easily in the global marketplace through zero or reduced tariffs and other provisions.

Key Benefits of Free Trade Agreements

FTA benefits for your product may require more record-keeping but can also give your product a competitive advantage versus products from other countries. U.S. FTAs typically address a wide variety of government activities that affect your business:

- Reduction or elimination of tariffs on qualified goods. For example, a country that normally charges a tariff of 12% of the value of the imported product will eliminate that tariff for products that originate (as defined in the FTA) in the United States. This makes your products competitive in the market.
- Intellectual Property Protection: protection and enforcement of American-owned intellectual property rights in the FTA partner country.
- Product Standards: the ability for U.S. exporters to participate in the development of product standards in the FTA partner country.
- Selling to the government: the ability for a U.S. company to bid on certain government procurements in the FTA partner country.
- Service companies: the ability for U.S. service suppliers to supply their services in the FTA partner country.
- Fair treatment for U.S. investors providing they be treated as favorably as the FTA partner country treats its own investors and their investments or investors and investments from any third country.

Industry and Product Classification

There are three standard classification systems for merchandise trade: The **Harmonized System (HS)**, the North American Industry Classification System (NAICS), and the Standard International Trade Classification (SITC). In addition, other classifications in use for trade statistics include End Use Commodity Category and Advanced Technology Products (ATP).

Harmonized System (HS Code)

The **Harmonized System** is an international classification system standardized between countries at a basic 6-digit level, with country-specific definitions for the 8- and 10-digit levels. It is used to classify physical goods. Commodity classifications in the U.S. are given in two publications, where Schedule B is for export.

- **Schedule B** - Export statistics are initially collected and compiled in terms of approximately 8,000 commodity classifications in Schedule B, Statistical Classification of Domestic and Foreign Commodities Exported from the United States, a publication of the U.S. Census Bureau and based on the Harmonized System. Schedule B is administered by the U.S. Census Bureau.

Why do you need an HS code?

The HS codes are used to calculate product tariffs (duty). They are required to fill out shipping documents (e.g., commercial invoices, packing lists, etc.) and facilitate the customs clearance process, preventing potential delays and compliance issues by providing a standardized way to identify your product internationally. There are several different types of tariffs. See more information on tariff resources. For useful resources to estimate duties and taxes visit **Tariff Fees Overview and Resources page**.

North American Industry Classification System (NAICS)

The North American Industry Classification System (NAICS) is a consistent system for economic analysis across the three North American Free Trade Agreement partners: Canada, Mexico, and the United States. NAICS is built on a production-oriented or supply-based conceptual framework in that establishments are grouped into industries according to similar processes used to produce goods or services. NAICS is a 6-digit hierarchical coding system.

Standard International Trade Classification (SITC)

A statistical classification of the commodities entering external trade designed to provide the commodity aggregates needed for purposes of economic analysis and to facilitate the international comparison of trade-by-commodity data.

End-Use Commodity Category

The US Harmonized Tariff System and Schedule B classification systems are summarized into six principals "end-use" categories and further subdivided into about 140 broad commodity groupings. These categories are used in developing seasonally adjusted and constant dollar totals. The concept of end-use demand was developed for balance of payments purposes by the Bureau of Economic Analysis.

Advanced Technology Products (ATP)

About 500 of some 22,000 commodity classification codes used in reporting U.S. merchandise trade are identified as "advanced technology" codes and they meet the following criteria:

- The code contains products whose technology is from a recognized high technology field (e.g. biotechnology).
- These products represent leading-edge technology in that field.
- Such products constitute a significant part of all items covered in the selected classification code.

This product and commodity-based measure of advanced technology differs from broader NAICS industry-based measures which include all goods produced by a particular industry group, regardless of the level of technology embodied in the goods.

Finding Qualified Buyers and Partners

Finding Buyers or Partners

Finding Foreign Buyers: Trade Missions

Looking for more opportunities to find foreign buyers or partners? As part of your export planning, consider joining a U.S. Department of Commerce trade mission. U.S. businesses are organized to travel to foreign countries, and are led by industry experts or senior officials.

U.S. Department of Commerce Organized Trade Missions

Each year, numerous U.S. companies participate in Department of Commerce organized trade missions. Leverage new trade leads, partnering opportunities, and international sales through these trade mission benefits:

- One-to-one meetings with foreign industry executives and government officials, pre-screened to match your specific business objectives whether for representation, direct sales or joint ventures in the local market.
- Networking events with guests from local industry multipliers including chambers of commerce, associations and business councils influential in the business community.
- Briefings and roundtables with the legal and business community on local business practices and opportunities.

- Site visits to local facilities where your technologies/services may be applied.
- Media coverage.

Finding Foreign Buyers: Trade Shows

Diversify your international selling strategy by either presenting your products at major foreign trade shows, or by meeting with foreign buyers at U.S. trade shows. The U.S. Commercial Service has many services to enhance your trade show experience.

Export Trade Show Programs

Develop new trade leads, partnering opportunities, and sales in your international selling strategies by leveraging U.S. Department of Commerce assistance at domestic and worldwide export trade shows. Below are examples of how to find international buyers through popular trade event programs:

International Buyer Program

- The International Buyer Program (IBP) supports major domestic trade shows featuring U.S. products and services with high export potential. U.S. Commercial Service trade experts located at U.S. embassies and consulates worldwide recruit prospective foreign buyers to attend selected trade shows, and match them with U.S. exhibitors.
- Along with networking opportunities, participating U.S. companies benefit from hands-on export counseling, marketing analysis, and matchmaking services by Commerce's country and industry experts.
- Each year, the IBP selects and promotes about 30 U.S. trade shows that attract an average of 13,000 foreign buyers. The result is hundreds of millions of dollars in new

business for U.S. exhibitors in a variety of leading industrial sectors.

Certified Trade Fairs

- Trade fairs are "shop windows" where thousands of companies from many countries display their goods and services. The fairs serve as a marketplace where buyers and sellers can meet with mutual convenience.
- Many trade fairs are certified by the U.S. Department of Commerce. The certified show/U.S. pavilion represents a U.S. Department of Commerce endorsement, ensuring a high-quality, multifaceted opportunity for American companies to successfully market overseas.
- At the U.S.-themed pavilion, U.S. Commercial Service trade professionals assist American businesses by facilitating access to foreign buyers, agents, and industry representatives. Services include pre-show industry/country market briefings, one-on-one export counseling, onsite promotion, and more. Each year, the U.S. Department of Commerce certifies some 100 events in more than 23 countries in a variety of industry sectors.

Foreign Agricultural Service (www.fas.usda.gov)

Through a network of counselors, attachés, trade officers, commodity analysts, and marketing specialists, the Department of Agriculture's Foreign Agricultural Service (FAS) can help arrange contacts overseas and provide marketing assistance for companies that export agricultural commodities.

International Company Profiles

An International Company Profile (ICP) is a background report on a specific foreign company that is prepared by commercial officers of the U.S. Commercial Service at American embassies and consulates.

These reports include:

- Information on the company
- Year established
- Relative size
- Number of employees
- General reputation
- Territory covered
- Language capabilities
- Product lines handled
- Principal owners
- Financial references
- Trade references

Each ICP also contains a general report by the U.S. Commercial Service officer who conducted the investigation concerning the reliability of the foreign company.

The ICP service is offered in countries that lack adequate private-sector providers of credit and background information on local companies. Credit reports on foreign companies are available from many private-sector sources, including (in the United States) Dun & Bradstreet and Graydon International.

International Partner Search

With the U.S. Commercial Service's International Partner Search, teams of experts in more than 75 countries work to find you the most suitable strategic partners. You provide your marketing materials and background on your company. The U.S. Commercial Service uses its strong network of international contacts to interview potential partners and to provide you with a list of up to five pre-screened companies. By working only with pre-screened companies that are interested in buying or selling your products and services, you save valuable time and money.

The International Partner Search allows you to obtain high-quality market information in 15 days. The search yields information on each potential partner's size, sales, years in business, and number of employees, as well as a statement from each potential partner on the marketability of your product or service. You will also receive complete contact information on key individuals among the potential partners who are interested in your company.

Plan Your Market Entry Strategy: Export Counseling

The U.S. Commercial Service has a global network of trade professionals with "boots-on-the-ground" expertise around the world. Services are varied and wide-ranging: trade experts can help with export planning, navigating customs and documentation issues, locating pre-screened overseas buyers, finding the best foreign export markets, trade show support, international market research, and more. To address other specific exporting needs, such as trade financing and risk mitigation, trade professionals work in partnership with agencies like U.S. Small Business Administration and U.S. Export-Import Bank.

Export Counseling

- Develop effective market entry and sales strategies.

- Understand export documentation requirements and import regulations of foreign markets.
- Navigate U.S. government export controls, compliance and trade financing options

Business Matchmaking

- Connect with pre-screened potential partners.
- Promote your product or service to prospective buyers at trade events worldwide.
- Meet with international industry and government decision makers in your target markets

Market Intelligence

- Analyze market potential and foreign competitors.
- Obtain useful information on best prospects, financing, laws, and cultural issues.
- Conduct background checks on potential buyers and distributors.

Commercial Diplomacy

- Overcome trade obstacles to successfully enter international markets.
- Benefit from coordinated U.S. government engagement with foreign governments to protect U.S. business interests.
- Access U.S. government trade advocacy for your foreign government procurement bids.

Other Ways to Find Buyers or Partners

Exporting your products to foreign markets can be a great way to grow your business and reach new customers.

Here are some tips from the search results:

1. Use online directories and search engines:

Online directories and search engines can help you locate international markets for your export product and connect with international buyers. You can use these platforms to find contact information for potential buyers and reach out to them directly.

2. Work with foreign agencies:

This is the most reliable way to find buyers for your export products is to work with a foreign import agency. Many countries have state managed trading companies that work through embassies from other countries.

3. Send emails or messages:

You can send emails or messages to genuine or potential buyers to introduce your product and start a conversation. Make sure to use effective references and links in your emails to gain the trust of buyers.

4. Online Overseas business:

e-commerce is B2B and B2C online sales, a term that covers everything a business does online to sell to consumers, both domestically and overseas. It includes:

- The sale through a website
- The online advertising that leads to a sale
- The brand building that helps tie it all together as a narrative for consumers.

5. Find and research on Social Media:

Facebook, LinkedIn and other social media groups can be a great way to get opinions from local people and ask about pricing and product opinion.

6. Build Relationships with Buyers:

Finding potential buyers is not enough; you also need to build trust and rapport with them. You should:

- Follow up with the buyers regularly and provide them with relevant information and updates:
- Answer their questions and address their concerns promptly and professionally.
- Provide them with samples, testimonials, or references if possible.
- Negotiate the terms and conditions of the sale, such as price, payment method, delivery time, warranty, etc.
- Sign a contract or agreement that specifies the details of the transaction.
- Deliver your product on time and in good condition.
- Ask for feedback and suggestions for improvement.

Online Directories to Find Overseas Buyers

There are several online directories that can help you find overseas buyers for your export business. Here are some of the best directories according to the search results:

1. Thomasnet: Thomas is a leading industrial sourcing and marketing platform that empowers North American manufacturers, distributors, and service providers to grow through data-driven product discovery and strategic marketing solutions.

2. Foreign Trade Online: This site has a user-friendly directory and other useful tools, such as a list of trade shows that you can search through and plenty of information about travel and inspections. This is also aiming to promote greater access to world markets for small and medium-sized enterprises (SMEs) and provide opportunities for SMEs to expand their capabilities and reach beyond their own borders.

3. Wholesale Central: This is a B2B directory of wholesalers and dropshippers. This is the leading B2B directory of wholesale suppliers and products. It offers powerful sourcing tools to help resellers find thousands of prescreened wholesalers, importers, distributors, dropshippers, and manufacturers.

4. International Trade Administration: The International Trade Administration offers customized services to help you find new buyers and partners.

5. The Foreign Agricultural Service (FAS): FAS partners with more than 70 cooperator groups representing a cross-section of the U.S. food and agricultural industry and manages a toolkit of trade promotion programs to help U.S. exporters develop and maintain markets for hundreds of products. FAS also supports U.S. agricultural exporters through export credit guarantee programs and other types of assistance.

6. Export Portal: Export Portal is a B2B e-commerce platform aiming to be a comprehensive international trade hub for Small and Medium - sized Enterprises (SMEs) and their counterparts. Through our free b2b marketplace, businesses can find new markets for their products and services, and expand their reach to a global audience. Our exclusive benefits include a variety of features and tools to help businesses succeed in international trade. It is an online platform that provides a single point of access to international markets for Small and Medium-sized Enterprises (SMEs) helping them enter or expand their operations with overseas partners. Thus, our members can confidently trade, network, and communicate with other verified companies and experts from all over the world.

7. The Global Trade Helpdesk (GTH): The Global Trade Helpdesk (GTH) is a multi-agency initiative jointly led by ITC, UNCTAD, and the WTO that aims to simplify market research for companies, and especially Micro, Small and Medium Enterprises (MSMEs), by integrating trade and business information into a single online portal.

8. Tradekey: This is a worldwide B2B online marketplace for the purchase and sale of assets and internet enterprises. It is a gathering place for owners of online enterprises to exchange assets, including clothing, mobile apps, electronics, furniture, chemicals, beauty and personal care, and many more. This site caters as a b2b online portal to entrepreneurs and modern small-company owners.

9. ExportHub: This is an international B2B marketplace working as an online selling platform specializing in facilitating trade between countries and resolving issues that businesses encounter when importing and exporting goods.

10. Global Source: Global Sources is an internationally recognized multichannel Online-to-Offline (O2O) sourcing platform to facilitate global trade.

11. IndiaMart: From here, you can find importers from India.

12. Kompass: This is a global directory for B2B, Useful for finding both buyers and suppliers internationally.

These online directories can help you find overseas buyers for your export business. However, it's important to research and evaluate each directory to determine which one is best suited for your business.

Legal Requirements and Registrations

Choose A Business Structure for Export from The U.S.

Sole proprietorship

A sole proprietorship is easy to form and gives you complete control of your business. You're automatically considered to be a sole proprietorship if you do business activities but don't register as any other kind of business.

Sole proprietorships do not produce a separate business entity. This means your business assets and liabilities are not separate from your personal assets and liabilities. You can be held personally liable for the debts and obligations of the business. Sole proprietors are still able to get a trade name. It can also be hard to raise money because you can't sell stock, and banks are hesitant to lend to sole proprietorships.

Sole proprietorships can be a good choice for low-risk businesses and owners who want to test their business idea before forming a more formal business.

Partnership

Partnerships are the simplest structure for two or more people to own a business together. There are two common kinds of partnerships: limited partnerships (LP) and limited liability partnerships (LLP).

Limited partnerships have only one general partner with unlimited liability, and all other partners have limited liability. The partners with limited liability also tend to have limited control over the company, which is documented in a partnership agreement. Profits are passed through to personal tax returns, and the general partner — the partner without limited liability — must also pay self-employment taxes.

Limited liability partnerships are similar to limited partnerships, but give limited liability to every owner. An LLP protects each partner from debts against the partnership, they won't be responsible for the actions of other partners.

Limited liability company (LLC)

An LLC lets you take advantage of the benefits of both the corporation and partnership business structures.

LLCs protect you from personal liability in most instances, your personal assets — like your vehicle, house, and savings accounts — won't be at risk in case your LLC faces bankruptcy or lawsuits.

Profits and losses can get passed through to your personal income without facing corporate taxes. However, members of an LLC are considered self-employed and must pay self-employment tax contributions towards Medicare and Social Security.

LLCs can have a limited life in many states. When a member joins or leaves an LLC, some states may require the LLC to be dissolved and re-formed with new membership — unless there's already an agreement in place within the LLC for buying, selling, and transferring ownership.

LLCs can be a good choice for medium- or higher-risk businesses, owners with significant personal assets they want protected, and owners who want to pay a lower tax rate than they would with a corporation.

Corporation

C corp

A corporation, sometimes called a C corp, is a legal entity that's separate from its owners. Corporations can make a profit, be taxed, and can be held legally liable.

Corporations offer the strongest protection to its owners from personal liability, but the cost to form a corporation is higher than other structures. Corporations also require more extensive record-keeping, operational processes, and reporting.

S corp

An S corporation, sometimes called an S corp, is a special type of corporation that's designed to avoid the double taxation drawback of regular C Corps. S corps allow profits, and some losses, to be passed through directly to owners' personal income without ever being subject to corporate tax rates.

Choose Your Business Name and Register It to Protect

You can choose a business name that reflects your brand identity and doesn't clash with the types of goods and services you offer. Once you settle on a name you like, you need to protect it. There are four different ways to register your business name. Each way of registering your name serves a different purpose, and some may be legally required depending on your business structure and location.

- Entity name protects you at a state level
- Trademark protects you at a federal level

- Doing business as (DBA) doesn't give legal protection, but it might be legally required
- Domain name protects your business website address

Each of these name registrations are legally independent. Most small businesses try to use the same name for each kind of registration, but you're not normally required to.

Register Your Business

Register with federal agencies

Many companies in the United States have to report information about their beneficial owners – the individuals who ultimately own or control the company. This report is made to the Financial Crimes Enforcement Network (FinCEN). FinCEN is a bureau of the U.S. Department of the Treasury. BOI reporting is a requirement of the Corporate Transparency Act of 2021.

Companies that are required to comply are called reporting companies. For additional information, refer to FinCEN's BOI notice (PDF).

Register with state agencies

If your business is a limited liability company (LLC), corporation, partnership, or nonprofit corporation, you'll probably need to register with any state where you conduct business activities.

Typically, you're considered to be conducting business activities in a state when:

- Your business has a physical presence in the state
- You often have in-person meetings with clients in the state
- A significant portion of your company's revenue comes from the state

- Any of your employees work in the state

Some states allow you to register online, and some states make you file paper documents in person or through the mail.

Register with local agencies

Typically, you don't need to register with county or city governments to actually form your business.

If your business is an LLC, corporation, partnership, or nonprofit corporation, you might need to file for licenses and permits from the county or city.

Some counties and cities also require you to register your DBA — a trade name or a fictitious name — if you use one.

Local governments determine registration, licensing, and permitting requirements, so visit local government websites to find out what you need to do.

Registering with The IRS for Getting an EIN

After business registration you need to register with the IRS (The Internal Revenue Service) for applying for an EIN (Employer Identification Number).

What is an EIN

The Employer Identification Number (EIN), often called a Federal Tax ID, is a nine-digit number that uniquely identifies your business for tax purposes. Think of it as a Social Security number for your company. Every business structure—whether a sole proprietorship, partnership, LLC, or corporation—may need an EIN, especially if it plans to hire employees, operates as a corporation or partnership, files employment, excise, or alcohol/tobacco/firearms tax returns, or withholds taxes for non-wage income paid to a non-resident alien.

Having an EIN is more than just a formality; it is essential to legitimizing and organizing your business. It enables you to open business bank accounts, establish business credit, hire employees, and comply with federal and state tax obligations. Additionally, you may need an EIN for contracts, vendor accounts, and even securing financing.

Preparing to file for an EIN

Before you file for an EIN, there are a few things you can do to prepare. First, determine your eligibility: to apply online for an EIN, your business must be physically located within the US or its territories. You must also be able to identify a responsible party, which is the person who controls, manages, or directs the business's day-to-day operations and has access to the business's funds. This person must have a valid Taxpayer Identification Number (TIN) such as an SSN, Individual Taxpayer Identification Number (ITIN), or an existing EIN.

If you meet these eligibility requirements, you'll need to gather the following information:

- The full legal name of your business and any trade names or "doing business as" (DBA) names.
- The mailing address and physical address of your business.
- Your entity type (e.g. corporation, LLC) and reason for applying for the EIN.
- Your business's primary activities and how many employees you expect to have in the first year.

How to Apply for an EIN

Applying for an EIN is straightforward, and you can accomplish it through several methods, including online, by mail, fax, or telephone (for international applicants). Here's how it works:

- **Applying Online**: The fastest and most straightforward way to obtain an EIN is through the IRS website's online EIN application system. The service is available Monday through Friday during specific hours. Upon completion of the online form, you will receive your EIN immediately. Be prepared to answer questions about your business, including its legal structure, reason for applying, and responsible party information.
- **Applying by Mail or Fax**: If you prefer a paper-based approach, you can complete Form SS-4 and mail or fax it to the IRS. Processing times may vary, with faxed applications generally being processed within four days, while mailed forms may take up to four weeks. This method is more common for those who need help to use the online application, such as overseas businesses.
- **Telephone Applications for International Applicants**: Non-U.S. applicants can apply for an EIN by calling the IRS's EIN International Desk. This is ideal for foreign entities with business operations in the United States. Be sure to have all the necessary information and be prepared to answer questions to verify your eligibility.

Using Your EIN

Once you receive your EIN, it's time to use it. Your EIN serves as your business's unique identifier and is essential for various functions.

- **Filing Federal Taxes**

You'll need your EIN when filing federal taxes. This number helps the IRS identify your business, track tax payments, and manage tax-related issues. Ensuring your EIN is used correctly in tax filings can prevent delays and compliance issues with the IRS.

Beyond simply identifying your business, an EIN allows you to claim relevant tax deductions and credits more effectively. It also helps streamline the process if your business is subject to audits or if you need to resolve any disputes related to your tax status.

- **Opening a Business Bank Account**

A separate business bank account is crucial for keeping your personal and business finances distinct. Most banks require an EIN to open a business bank account. This distinction simplifies bookkeeping and makes it easier to track your business's income and expenses, which is invaluable come tax season.

By opening a business bank account with your EIN, you can access various financial tools and services tailored for businesses, such as specialized business loans, credit lines, and merchant services. These benefits make managing and scaling your business more seamless.

- **Applying for Business Credit**

Your EIN also plays a role in building business credit. Lenders and credit agencies use your EIN to assess your business's creditworthiness. Establishing business credit can help secure loans, negotiate better terms with suppliers, and open growth opportunities.

Developing a solid business credit profile with your EIN gives you access to better financing terms and shields your personal credit.

This separation ensures that any challenges your business faces won't directly impact your credit standing, giving you more financial security.

- **Completing Employee Payroll**

If you have or plan to have employees, your EIN will be necessary for payroll purposes. It reports employment taxes, including Social Security and Medicare taxes. Accurate use of your EIN ensures compliance with federal regulations and maintains a professional standing with your employees.

Additionally, your EIN allows you to provide accurate and timely tax documents to your employees, such as W-2 forms. This promotes transparency and trust within your workforce, reducing the risk of potential penalties for misreported employee wages.

Conclusion

Registering your business with the IRS and obtaining an EIN is essential in solidifying your operation's legal standing and opening new growth opportunities. By understanding the process and taking advantage of available resources, you can navigate the registration process confidently. An EIN is more than a tax ID—it is a gateway to greater credibility, compliance, and capability as you build and expand your business.

Export Licenses

What is an Export License?

An export license is a vital shipping document issued by government agencies that authorize the trade of certain goods across US borders.

Note:

- Not all exports require a license. Before shipping, check with the relevant agency for goods that require a permit/license to carry out the trade.
- The issuing agency for export licenses varies depending on the type of goods you're dealing in.
- The export license has limited validity, typically 4 years if the Bureau of Industry and Security issues it.

How to apply for a US export license?

The International Trade Administration (ITA) states that 95% of US exports don't require an export license. So, before exporting, it's imperative to identify whether your goods need a license.

Export license/permit requirement depends on several factors, such as:

- The item being exported (product or technology).
- Where it is exported.
- Who is the consignee?
- What's the intended usage of the shipped item?

Here's how you can apply for an export license in the US:

Step 1: Determine if your goods require an export license

- Research the composition and end-use of the product you're exporting. Based on that, see whether it falls in the licensing category.
- The ITA maintains a Consolidated Screening List. You need an export license if you export to any of the parties or entities mentioned in the list.
- If your exported goods fall under the Export Administration Regulations jurisdiction (EAR), you need to

obtain an export license from the Bureau of Industry and Security.

Step 2: Check for other license requirements

Apart from EAR, other Partner Government Agencies may also require a license for certain types of exported goods. For example:

- The International Traffic in Arms Regulations may have license or permit requirements for defense goods or services.
- The Office of Foreign Assets Control maintains a list of people/entities subject to some trade restrictions based on foreign policies. Depending on who you export to, you may need an export license. The OFAC entities are also listed on the Consolidated Screening List.
- The Nuclear Regulatory Commission and Food and Drug Administration also administer export controls.

Note: Obtain the required export license from the concerned agency's website.

Step 3: Submit your export license application

Is your company registered with BIS and has a Company Identification Number (CIN)?

- Yes: Great, you can directly apply for an export license through the Simplified Network Application Processing (SNAP-R) portal by BIS.
- No: Don't worry! You can register your company and obtain the CIN online. Then, proceed with the SNAP-R portal to apply for a license.

Documents required for US export licenses

Some essential documents required for obtaining an export license in the U.S. include:

- Employer Identification Number (EIN): Obtained from the IRS.
- Dun & Bradstreet Number (D-U-N-S): A unique 9-digit identification number assigned to businesses by Dun and Bradstreet (D&B); government agencies recognize it as a standard identifier for a specific business entity.
- Incorporation or business registration documents: Proof that your business is legally registered and operating in the U.S.
- Product information: Such as Harmonized Tariff Schedule (HTS) codes and country of origin for the products you plan to export.
- End-use statement: A statement outlining the intended use of the exported goods.
- Broker's license: If you use a customs broker for your exports, they need to have a valid customs broker license.
- Power of attorney: If you plan to authorize someone else to act on your behalf during the licensing process. Other shipping documents include the bill of lading, commercial invoice, inspection certificate, CBP entry form, and relevant certificates from relevant Partner Government Agencies (PGAs).

Other shipping documents include the bill of lading, commercial invoice, inspection certificate, CBP entry form, and relevant certificates from relevant Partner Government Agencies (PGAs).

Note: Depending on the type of goods being imported or exported and the regulations of the country of destination, additional documentation may be required. It's always best to check with the concerned authorities to ensure you have all the necessary documents before starting the process.

Export Compliance and Documentation

Export Administration Regulations (EAR)

The Export Administration Regulations (EAR) set the rules for exporting items that could threaten U.S. national security and foreign policy. For businesses, especially those manufacturing regulated products, understanding EAR is crucial. Proper compliance involves correctly classifying items, knowing when export licenses are required, and using applicable exceptions. This not only helps avoid heavy fines and loss of export privileges but also ensures sensitive technologies are handled lawfully, which ultimately helps to protect international trade relationships and maintain security.

The EAR are U.S. laws that set the rules and regulations for exporting and re-exporting commercial and "dual-use" items (i.e., things with both commercial and military applications). For example, software used for data encryption could be used in everyday business operations but also in military settings for secure communication.

The EAR are issued by the United States Department of Commerce, Bureau of Industry and Security (BIS) under laws relating to the control of certain exports, reexports, and activities.

Who needs to comply with EAR?

Those in the following sectors need to comply with EAR due to the type of products and technologies they produce and export:

- **Tech and electronics.** These companies often produce computer software, hardware, and telecommunications equipment.
- **Aviation and aerospace.** This sector deals with navigation systems and aircraft parts, which have obvious military applications.
- **Biological and chemical.** Manufacturers in this field may handle substances and biological agents that could be used in weapons development.
- **Manufacturing and engineering.** This includes businesses that produce machinery and industrial equipment that can be used to develop weapons and other tools that can serve a military use case.
- **Research and development.** R&D entities often develop advanced technologies (think artificial intelligence) with commercial and potential military uses.

How does the EAR classification system work?

The BIS relies on a classification system that categorizes dual-use items using Export Control Classification Numbers (ECCNs) listed on the Commerce Control List (CCL). Each ECCN identifies the level of control required based on the nature of the item and its final destination.

These classifications help determine whether you need an export license for a specific item. For example, if you're exporting data encryption software, it might fall under a particular ECCN that requires a license, especially if it's getting sent to a country with strict export controls.

What items does EAR apply to?

It's important to note that this set of regulations covers a diverse range of items, including software, electronics, and chemicals.

1. **Dual-use items.** Goods, software, and technology with commercial and military applications.
2. **Commercial items.** These are products that are not specifically designed for military use but could have military applications.
3. **Items of U.S. origin**. Any item produced in the U.S., including foreign-made items that contain U.S. components or technology above a de Minimis level.
4. **Certain foreign-made items.** Products made outside the country that contain more than a de Minimis amount of materials made in the U.S.

What are the EAR license exceptions?

EAR allows businesses to export certain items without a license under specific conditions. Some key exceptions include:

- **Low-Value Shipments (LVS).** EAR allows for the export of some low-value items without a license if they don't exceed a specific dollar value threshold for their assigned ECCN and destination. For example, exporting electronic components worth less than $2,500 to certain countries might qualify under LVS.
- **Technology and Software Restricted (TSR).** This exception permits the export of software and technology to countries listed as eligible under this exception, such as some Western European countries, without a license. This exception typically applies to less sensitive items under EAR.

- **Encryption Commodities, Software, and Technology (ENC).** Businesses can export encryption products under specific circumstances without a license, provided they meet defined technical specifications and reporting requirements. For example, mass-market encryption software might be exported to non-embargoed countries under ENC.

EAR compliance checklist

Staying compliant with the Export Administration Regulations is crucial for any business dealing with sensitive technologies. Here's a simple checklist to help you navigate EAR compliance and protect your company from potential penalties:

- Determine your product classifications

Start by identifying whether your products are considered "dual-use" items, meaning they have both commercial and military applications. Use the ECCNs on the CCL to accurately classify your items. This mandatory first step will help you better understand what controls apply to your products.

- Understand your licensing requirements

Each ECCN outlines the controls based on the nature of the item and where it's going. Check if an export license is needed by considering the ECCN, destination country, end-user, and intended use of the item. For example, exporting certain encryption software may require a specific license, depending on where and how it will be used.

- Check for license exceptions

Some exports may qualify for license exceptions under the EAR, which can save time and reduce paperwork. Each exception has its own criteria based on the item, destination, and end-use. Make sure you fully understand these exceptions to avoid unauthorized exports.

- Implement a compliance strategy

Establish internal policies, training, and procedures to ensure all staff understand and abide by EAR requirements. It's particularly important to set the proper access control measures in place to comply with the Deemed Export Rule under EAR, which refers to the sharing of controlled technology or software source code to a foreign national within the United States. Under this provision, the "deemed export" is treated as if the technology or software were exported to the foreign national's home country. As a result, you may need an export license depending on the technology's classification and the foreign national's country of origin.

- Maintain accurate records

Under EAR, businesses are required to maintain detailed documentation of export transactions, licensing, and compliance efforts for at least five years. This thorough record-keeping will come in handy in case of an audit or investigation. Accurate records help prove that your exports were conducted legally and in accordance with EAR rules.

- Schedule internal audits

Conducting internal audits on a regular basis will help you ensure that your compliance processes align with EAR requirements. These audits help identify gaps in your procedures, verify that records are accurate, and ensure that your staff stays current on compliance practices and regulatory updates.

- Report violations immediately

If you discover any violations, report them to the BIS right away. Self-reporting can often lead to reduced penalties and shows that your company is proactive about correcting issues and improving compliance processes.

- Stay updated on regulatory changes

EAR is frequently updated to reflect new technologies, threats, and shifts in U.S. policy. Updates could involve changes to the CCL, reclassification of items, country-specific restrictions, or new licensing requirements. All in all, regular monitoring helps businesses ensure compliance and avoid legal and financial consequences.

Schedule B Codes and Product Classification

What Are Schedule B Codes?

The Schedule B code is a U.S.-specific coding system administered by the International Trade Management Division of the U.S. Census Bureau to monitor U.S. exports. These codes take the same form as HS codes for the first six digits, but include four additional digits for a total of 10 numbers. These additional numbers provide a more detailed product classification.

While similar in structure, Schedule B codes are not the same as Harmonized Tariff Schedule (HTS) codes, which are used for imports. Exporters should prioritize identifying the correct Schedule B code for their products, and it's the classification used for Electronic Export Information (EEI) that you submit to AESDirect.

Here's when you're required to report a Schedule B code through AESDirect:

- When the value of your goods per Schedule B number exceeds $2,500
- When your product requires an export license
- When exporting a used vehicle
- When exporting to China, Russia, or Venezuela, regardless of value (as of Sept. 27, 2020)

If you pay your freight forwarder or some other third party to file on your behalf, you should include the Schedule B code on your Shipper's Letter of Instruction (SLI) that you give them.

Here's a summary of Schedule B codes:

- Contain 10 digits
- Used exclusively in the United States and exclusively for exports
- May differ from the HTS codes used for imports

Schedule B Search Engine

In order to better assist exporters in providing more accurate trade statistics and filers in determining their correct export commodity code (Schedule B number), International Trade provides a Schedule B Commodity Search Tool. This search tool provides a smarter, more intuitive, and more accurate way to classify products. It understands and interprets common commercial product information, and interacts intelligently and intuitively with users to eliminate classification complexity. The search tool has cut down on the time it takes to classify products and provide more accurate and consistent results that ultimately improves the quality of trade statistics.

What is an HS number (HS code)?

The Harmonized System Classification is a standardized numerical method of classifying traded products. **HS numbers** (or HS codes) are used by customs authorities around the world to identify products for the assessing duties and taxes, among other things. HS codes are generally 10-digit long. However, governments harmonize (overlap) the HS codes up to the first six digits. Additional digits are added to the HS number by governments to further distinguish products in certain categories. Tip: You may want to think of an HS code as an "export code."

Is there a difference between HS and Schedule B numbers?

Yes. The HS number is an internationally accepted code. The basic HS code contains 6-digits, known as a subheading. The Schedule B is a 10-digit code built upon the first 6 digits of the HS code. Additionally, the Schedule B code is a U.S.-specific coding system used to monitor U.S. exports (e.g., for export compliance and trade data collection).

> **HTS codes**, also called **HTS** numbers, are administered by the U.S. International Trade Commission (ITC). The U.S. HTS codes are used for classifying products imported into the United States. Tip: Think of the HTS code as the U.S. "import code."

Exporters need to know their product classification, i.e., Schedule B and HS numbers for many reasons including:

- Classifying physical goods for shipment to a foreign country;

- Determining import tariff (duty) rates and figuring out if a product qualifies for a preferential tariff under a Free Trade Agreement (HS number);
- Filing the Electronic Export Information (EEI);
- Completing shipping documents, such as shipper's letter of instructions, commercial invoice or certificate of origin. (HS number);
- Conducting market research including analyzing trade statistics.

What Is AESDirect and How to Fill EEI

Introduction to the Automated Export System (AES)

Before AES, the export system was paper-bound; expensive, labor intensive, error prone. AES uses proven technology in a new way to address a significant problem with the export process. It will contribute to a re-engineering of the way U.S. exports are accomplished. The Automated Export System (AES) is a joint venture between CBP, the Foreign Trade Division of the Bureau of the Census (Commerce), the Bureau of Industry and Security (Commerce), the Directorate of Defense Trade Controls (State), other federal agencies, and the export trade community.

It is the central point through which export shipment data required by multiple agencies is filed electronically to CBP, using the efficiencies of Electronic Data Interchange (EDI). AES provides an alternative to filing paper Electronic Export Information (EEI). Export information is collected electronically and edited immediately, and errors are detected and corrected at the time of filing. AES is a nationwide system operational at all ports and for all methods of transportation. It was designed to assure compliance with and enforcement of laws relating to exporting, improve trade statistics, reduce duplicate reporting to multiple agencies, and improve customer service.

ACE AESDirect

The Automated Commercial Environment (ACE) AESDirect is the primary filing tool for submitting your Electronic Export Information (EEI) to the Automated Export System (AES). When a filer submits their EEI, the AES will process the information and, if accepted, respond with an Internal Transaction Number (ITN).

Electronic Export Information (EEI)

This electronic filing is referred to as Electronic Export Information (EEI) filing and is required when the value of the commodity classified under each individual Schedule B number is over $2,500, or if there exists a mandatory filing requirement, i.e., an export license is required. The EEI is submitted to the Automated Export System (AESDirect) hosted on the Automated Commercial Environment (ACE) platform. The exporter is responsible for preparing the EEI and the carrier files it with U.S. Customs and Border Protection through the AES or AES Direct.

EEI Filing Requirements

Filing of the EEI is required regardless of value or destination for the following shipments:

- valued over $2,500 per Schedule B number and is sent from one exporter to one buyer on one calendar day on one carrier; (According to the FTR Section 30.1(c), value is defined as the selling price in U.S. dollars plus inland and domestic freight, insurance, and other charges to the U.S. seaport, airport, or land border port of export);

- requiring an export license, regardless of value or destination;
- subject to the ITAR even if they are exempt from export licensing requirements regardless of value or destination;
- falling under "600 series" of the Export Control Classification Number (ECCN) for items enumerated in paragraphs "a to x";
- requiring license Exception-Strategic Trade Authorization (STA);
- destined for Cuba, Iran, North Korea, Sudan, or Syria (regardless of value);
- rough diamonds, regardless of value (HTS 7102.10, 7102.21 and 7102.31) and destination;
- used self-propelled vehicles;

Tips

If the exporter is sending baggage or containers with their personal or household goods valued over $2,500 to a foreign destination, other than Canada, they must file the EEI and provide the ITN to the carrier in accordance with the timeline.

If the exporter is sending goods through the U.S. Postal Service, they are required to file the EEI when the value of the commodity classified under each individual Schedule B number is over $2,500, or if the export requires a mandatory EEI filing requirement (see above). The exporter should submit the ITN or EEI filing exemption citation to the post office, if applicable.

EEI Filing Exemptions

- When the value of the commodity classified under each individual Schedule B number is $2,500 or less and mandatory EEI filing is not required.
- Shipments FROM the U.S. to Canada of ANY amount and mandatory EEI filing are not required.
- Shipments TO U.S. possessions, except those territories where EEI filing is required, i.e., between the US and Puerto Rico and from the US to the US Virgin Islands).

Tips

If your shipment is exempt from the EEI filing requirements, you must annotate the commercial document, i.e., air waybill, bill of loading, and invoice with the exemption citation. Annotate "NOEEI" followed by the Foreign Trade Regulation citation, i.e., "NOEEI 30.37(a)" for shipments when the value of each individual Schedule B number is $2,500 or less; "NOEEI; 30.36" for shipments to Canada, etc.

Who can do the EEI Filing

The filer of EEI for export transactions is either the USPPI, or the U.S. authorized agent. All EEI submitted to the AES shall be complete, correct, and based on personal knowledge of the facts stated or on information furnished by the parties to the export transaction. The filer shall be physically located in the United States at the time of filing, have an EIN or DUNS and be certified to report in the AES. In the event that the filer does not have an EIN or DUNS, the filer must obtain an EIN from the Internal Revenue Service.

You may file your EEI for your export transaction by accessing the ACE secure data portal located on the U.S. Customs and Border

Protection's website. First-time users will need to create an account and obtain a username and password prior to filing.

To learn more about the EEI filing in the AES, note these resources:

You may file your EEI for your export transaction by accessing the ACE secure data portal located on the U.S. Customs and Border Protection's website. First-time users will need to create an account and obtain a username and password prior to filing.

Filing Electronic Export Information (EEI) to get Internal Transaction Number (ITN)

Do you need to receive an ITN but aren't sure how to get started? You may file the Electronic Export Information (EEI) yourself to receive an ITN or have an Authorized Agent file on your behalf. If you choose to file yourself through the ACE website, below are four quick steps to create an Exporter Account and get started on ACE AESDirect:

1) In order to register on ACE, you must first receive an Employer Identification Number (EIN) if you do not have one already. Receiving the EIN requires a US Social Security Number and a US physical address. During the registration process you will be asked for a company name and company address. If you are an individual (i.e., not with a company), simply use your personal name and personal address. This must be an address in the United States.

2) Once you receive the EIN, complete the ACE Exporter Registration Form and submit. You will then receive a confirmation email containing a Username (Account ID) and Temporary Password.

3) After obtaining your Username and Temporary Password, go to the ACE website and click on "Trade/PGA User Login". Then click "Create an Account". The website will ask you to enter your First Name, Last Name, Email and Password (This is a new password that you create). Once you click 'Sign Up', the ACE Website will prompt you to enter the Username and Temporary Password from the email you received previously. This will link your Modernized ACE account to your Legacy ACE account.

4) Once signed in to the ACE website, select "Exporter" under the "Accounts" drop-down menu. Select the appropriate Exporter account by clicking the hyperlink for the account under the "Account Name" column. On the right side of the screen, select "Submit AES Filing" to launch AESDirect. Please ensure the pop-up blocker in your web browser is completely disabled.

If this is your first time accessing the ACE AESDirect portal, you must agree to the Certification Statements to proceed. Once in the portal, click 'Create Export Filing' and complete the EEI to obtain an ITN.

Essential Export Documents

Pro Forma Invoice

A pro forma invoice is an important document used as a negotiating tool between the seller and the buyer prior to an export shipment. This document should be used by the seller to quote at the beginning of an export transaction and it will eventually become the final commercial invoice used when goods are cleared through customs in the importing country. The document contains a description of goods (e.g., quantity, price, weight, kind, and other specifications) and is a declaration by the seller to provide the products and services to the buyer at the specified date and price.

Commercial Invoice

The commercial invoice is a legal document between the exporter and the buyer (in this case, the foreign buyer) that clearly states the goods being sold and the amount the customer is to pay. The commercial invoice is one of the main documents used by customs in determining customs duties. A commercial invoice is a bill for the goods from the seller to the buyer. These documents are often used by governments to determine the true value of goods when assessing customs duties. Governments that use the commercial invoice to control imports will often specify its form, content, number of copies, language to be used and other characteristics.

Packing List

Considerably more detailed and informative than a standard domestic packing list, an export packing list lists seller, buyer, shipper, invoice number, date of shipment, mode of transport, carrier, and itemizes quantity, description, type of package, such as a box, crate, drum, or carton, the number of packages, total net and gross weight (in kilograms), package marks and dimensions, if appropriate. Both commercial stationers and freight forwarders carry packing list forms. A packing list may serve as a conforming document. It is not a substitute for a commercial invoice. In addition, U.S. and foreign customs officials may use the packing list to check the cargo so the commercial invoice should reflect the information shown on the packing list.

Bill of Lading/Air Waybill

A bill of lading is a contract between the owner of the goods and the carrier (as with domestic shipments). For ocean shipments, there are two common types: a straight bill of lading, which is non-negotiable, and a negotiable, or shipper's order bill of lading. The latter can be used to buy, sell, or trade the goods while in transit. The customer usually needs an original bill of lading as proof of ownership to take possession of the goods from the ocean carrier. Air freight shipments require airway bills. An airway bill accompanies goods shipped by an international air carrier. The document provides detailed information about the shipment and allows it to be tracked. Air waybills are shipper-specific and are not negotiable documents (as opposed to "order" bills of lading used for vessel shipments).

Certificates of Origin (COO)

Required by some countries. A signed statement as to the origin of the export item. Certificates of origin are usually validated by a semiofficial organization, such as a local chamber of commerce. A certificate may be required even if the commercial invoice contains the same information or to comply with the requirements of foreign customs (i.e., country of importation), for letters of credit, or simply at the request of the buyer. There are two types of COOs: One type is known as "generic" or "non-preferential," which means that the country of origin of the goods stated on the document does not qualify the goods for any preferential treatment with the country on the receiving end. A second type of certificate may be required to obtain a free trade agreement (FTA) preferential tariff rate.

Electronic Export Information (EEI)

This electronic filing is referred to as Electronic Export Information (EEI) filing and is required when the value of the commodity classified under each individual Schedule B number is over $2,500, or if there exists a mandatory filing requirement, i.e., an export license is required. The EEI is submitted to the Automated Export System (AESDirect) hosted on the Automated Commercial Environment (ACE) platform.

Shipper's Letter of Instruction (SLI)

The Shipper's Letter of Instruction (SLI) is a formal document that conveys an exporter's instructions so there are no misunderstandings between the exporter and the freight forwarder who helps get their goods to foreign markets. A required export document in the U.S., the SLI is typically prepared by the exporter then provided to their freight forwarder.

The freight forwarder uses the information in the SLI for multiple purposes beyond where the goods are leaving from and arriving to – it provides them with an understanding of the weights and dimensions of the cargo to ensure its packed correctly to minimize damage, contains information required for an Automated Export System (AES) export filing, and enables them to prepare the Bill of Lading.

Insurance Certificate

Insurance certificates are used to assure the consignee that insurance will cover the loss of or damage to the cargo during transit. These can be obtained from your freight forwarder or publishing house. Note: an airway bill can serve as an insurance certificate for a shipment by air. Some countries may require certification or notification.

Shipping and Logistics

Choosing The Right Shipping Method

Selecting the optimal shipping method is crucial for efficient and cost-effective international shipping. Here's a breakdown of the primary options:

1. Sea Freight

Best for Large shipments, low-value goods, and non-urgent deliveries.

Pros: Cost-effective for large quantities, suitable for heavy and bulky items.

Cons: Longer transit times than air freight, the potential for delays due to port congestion.

2. Air Freight

Best for High-value, time-sensitive, or perishable goods.

Pros: Faster delivery times, suitable for urgent shipments.

Cons: More expensive than sea freight, limited cargo capacity.

3. Courier Services

Best for Small packages, documents, and urgent shipments.

Pros: Door-to-door delivery, tracking capabilities, and additional services like customs clearance.

Cons: More expensive than sea or air freight for larger shipments.

Factors to Consider When Choosing a Shipping Method:

Product Value: High-value items may benefit from faster, more secure air freight.

Delivery Time: Urgent shipments may require air freight, while less time-sensitive goods can be shipped by sea.

Shipment Size and Weight: The size and weight of your shipment will influence the most cost-effective method.

Product Sensitivity: Perishable or fragile goods may require specialized handling and temperature-controlled shipping.

Budget: Consider the cost of each shipping method and balance it with delivery time and insurance needs.

Additional Tips:

Choose a Reliable Shipping Partner: Select a reputable shipping company with experience in international shipping.

Proper Packaging: Ensure your goods are securely packaged to withstand the rigors of transportation.

Precise and Accurate Documentation: Prepare all necessary customs documents to avoid delays and penalties.

Insurance: Consider purchasing adequate insurance coverage to protect your shipment against loss or damage.

Track Your Shipment: Use tracking services to monitor the progress of your shipment.

By carefully considering these factors and selecting the appropriate shipping method, you can ensure that your goods reach their destination safely, efficiently, and cost-effectively.

Incoterms (International Commercial Terms)

What are Incoterms?

Incoterms are a collection of rules that are used to make shipping contracts and trade agreements between parties across the world. Incoterms clearly identify the responsibilities of each party, during every stage of the shipping process. Responsibilities can include costs, risks, who handles transport, etc.

Classes of Incoterms

Incoterms are updated by the ICC every 10 years, so the current set of Incoterms are known as Incoterms® 2020. Within the Incoterms, there are various categories of rules based on modes of transport. These classes are often identified via their acronyms.

Air, Sea, & Truck

- **EXW (Ex Works):** The buyer takes responsibility for all transport costs from the seller's location. This is often the lowest price quotation, as it doesn't include shipping.
- **FCA (Free Carrier):** The seller delivers the goods to a carrier or another party nominated by the buyer, at the seller's premises or another named place. Once the goods are handed over at that point, risk and responsibility transfer from seller to buyer.
- **CPT (Carriage Paid to):** The seller pays for the transportation of goods to a named destination, but the risk transfers to the buyer as soon as the goods are handed over to the first carrier.
- **CIP (Carriage & Insurance Paid to):** It is similar to CPT but includes an additional requirement. The seller must provide insurance coverage for the goods during transit.
- **DAP (Delivered at Place):** The seller takes responsibility for delivering goods to the buyer's location, excluding customs clearance.
- **DPU (Delivered at Place Unloaded):** The seller is responsible for the delivering the goods to a named destination and unloading them there, bearing all costs and risks until that point.

- **DDP (Delivered Duty Paid):** The seller delivers the goods to the buyer at the agreed destination and pays all costs, including duties and taxes, making it a highly buyer-friendly option.

Sea/Waterway Only

- **CFR (Cost & Freight):** The seller arranges and pays for transportation of goods to the port of destination, but the risk transfers to the buyer once the goods are loaded onto the ship.
- **CIF (Cost, Insurance, Freight):** The seller covers costs, insurance and freight to the buyer's port. This is a complete price for delivery to the port, appealing for buyers seeking minimal logistics management.
- **FAS (Free Alongside Ship):** The seller delivers the goods alongside the vessel at the named port of shipment. From that point onward, the buyer assumes all risks and costs, including loading, ocean freight, insurance and import customs clearance.
- **FOB (Free On Board):** The seller covers costs until the goods are loaded onto the vessel. The buyer is responsible for ocean freight, insurance and destination charges.

Incoterms Considerations

- When the goods you export arrive at their destination, the importing country requires that all applicable tariffs (import taxes levied by the destination country) and local taxes, including value-added tax (VAT), be paid. Many companies require the buyer to pay these tariffs and taxes.

- Buyers typically want to know the final price, with shipping and taxes included (known as the "landed cost"), before they agree to buy, but you might not be able to provide it—tariffs and taxes vary widely throughout the world, so determining those rates before you ship can be difficult. Be clear about your policy on tariffs—specifically, who pays and when payment will be due.
- The shipping companies you select often act as freight forwarders, helping you complete shipping documents, helping you estimate duties and taxes, pre-paying them for you, and then invoicing you. If you use the U.S. Postal Service for lighter weight shipments, its local partner in the buyer's country will collect duties and taxes.

Freight Forwarders and Customs Brokers

Freight Forwarders:

International freight forwarders are agents for exporters and can move cargo from "dock-to-door," providing several significant services:

- Arranging for and tracking of freight from a domestic and international perspective;
- Arranging for and tracking inland transportation;
- Preparation of shipping and export documents;
- Warehousing;
- Booking cargo space;
- Negotiating freight charges;
- Freight consolidation;

- Cargo insurance

Most freight forwarders are also non-vessel operating common carriers (NVOCCs) as well. Both freight forwarders and NVOCCs are licensed and regulated by the Federal Maritime Commission.

Customs Brokers:

Customs brokers assist importers in meeting federal requirements governing imports into the United States. Brokers are private individuals, partnerships, associations or corporations licensed, regulated and empowered by U.S. Customs and Border Protection (CBP). Customs brokers oversee transactions related to customs entry and admissibility of merchandise, product classification, customs valuation, payment of duties, taxes, or other charges such as refunds, rebates, and duty drawbacks. There are approximately 11,000 active licensed customs brokers in the United States.

Packaging and Labeling

Packaging

Your company should be aware of the demands that international shipping puts on packaged goods. You should also keep four potential problems in mind when designing an export shipping crate: breakage, moisture, pilferage, and excess weight. Buyers are often familiar with the port systems overseas, so they will sometimes specify packaging requirements. If the buyer does not provide such specifications, be sure the goods are prepared using these guidelines:

- Pack in strong containers that are adequately sealed and filled when possible.

- Make sure the weight is evenly distributed to provide proper bracing in the container, regardless of size.
- Put goods on pallets and, when possible, place them in containers.
- Make packages and packing filler out of moisture-resistant material.
- To avoid pilferage, avoid writing contents or brand names on packages.
- Use straps, seals, and shrink-wrap to safeguard goods.
- Observe any product-specific hazardous materials packing requirements.
- Verify compliance with wood-packaging documentation and markings for fumigation and chemical treatment.

One popular method of shipment is to use containers obtained from carriers or private leasing companies. These containers vary in size, material, and construction. They accommodate most cargo but are best suited for standard package sizes and shapes. Also, refrigerated and liquid-bulk containers are usually readily available. Some containers are no more than semitrailers lifted off their wheels, placed on a vessel at the port of export, and then transferred to another set of wheels at the port of import.

Labeling

Export shipping cartons and containers have specific markings and labeling that:

- Meet shipping regulations
- Ensure proper handling
- Conceal the identity of the contents

- Help receivers identify shipments
- Ensure compliance with environmental and safety standards

The overseas buyer usually specifies which export marks should appear on the cargo for easy identification by receivers. Products may require many markings for shipment. For example, exporters need to put the following markings on cartons to be shipped:

- Shipper's mark
- Country of origin (in your case, "U.S.A.")
- Weight marking (in pounds and kilograms)
- Number of packages and size of cases (in inches and centimeters)
- Handling marks (i.e., international pictorial symbols)
- Cautionary markings, such as "This Side Up" or "Use No Hooks" (in English and in the language of the destination country)
- Port of entry
- Labels for hazardous materials (i.e., universal symbols adopted by the International Air Transport Association and the International Maritime Organization)
- Ingredients (if applicable, also included in the language of the destination country)

Consumers are concerned with both the product itself and the product's secondary features, such as packaging, warranties, and services. Branding and labeling products in foreign markets raise new considerations for your company, such as:

- Are international brand names important to promote and distinguish a product? Conversely, should local brands or private labels be used to heighten local interest?
- Are the colors used on labels and packages offensive or attractive to the foreign buyer? For example, in some countries certain colors are associated with death.
- Can labels and instructions be produced in official or customary languages if required by law or practice?
- Does information on product content and country of origin have to be provided?
- Are weights and measures stated in the local unit? Even with consumer products, packaging and describing contents in metric measurements (e.g., kilograms, liters) can be important.
- Must each item be labeled individually? What is the language of the labeling? For example, "Made in the U.S." may not be acceptable; the product may need to be labeled in the language spoken by the country's consumers. There may be special labeling requirements for foods, pharmaceuticals, and other products.
- Are local tastes and knowledge considered? A cereal box with the picture of a U.S. athlete on it may not be as attractive to overseas consumers as the picture of a local sports hero.

Your U.S. brand name is important to you, but it may be less important to foreign consumers. On the other hand, in some places, it may be more valuable than it is in the U.S.

A visible endorsement from a famous person may get sales at home, but the same person may be unknown-or, worse, disliked-elsewhere.

Cargo Insurance

Damaging weather conditions, rough handling by carriers, and other common hazards to cargo make insurance of shipments an important protection for U.S. exporters. Your shipper or freight forwarder will contract with an insurance company to cover the goods you export.

If the terms of sale make you responsible for insurance, your company should either obtain its own policy or insure the cargo under a freight forwarder's policy for a fee. If the terms of sale make the foreign buyer responsible, you should not assume (or even take the buyer's word) that adequate insurance has been obtained. If the buyer neglects to obtain adequate coverage, damage to the cargo may cause a major financial loss to your company. Shipments by sea are covered by marine cargo insurance. Air shipments may also be covered by marine cargo insurance, or insurance may be purchased from the air carrier.

Export shipments are usually covered by cargo insurance against loss, damage, and delay in transit. International agreements often limit carrier liability. Additionally, the coverage is substantially different from domestic coverage. Arrangements for insurance may be made by either the buyer or the seller in accordance with the terms of sale. Exporters are advised to consult with international insurance carriers or freight forwarders for more information. Although sellers and buyers can agree to different components,

coverage is usually placed at 110 percent of the CIF (cost, insurance, freight) or CIP (carriage and insurance paid to) value.
A second kind of insurance, however, also is recommended: The sale must be insured against nonpayment. The buyer's lender and other financial institutions named in your sale terms increasingly require credit insurance to cover risks of nonpayment. Contingencies include default by buyer or lender, political causes, or foreign currency disasters that put your payment at risk.

Financial Considerations and Payment

Key Cost Components to Start Export Business

Starting an export business from the U.S., even with a focus on low capital, involves a range of cost components. These can vary significantly based on your business model (e.g., dropshipping vs. holding inventory), the type of product, target market and your willingness to leverage free government resources and Do It Yourself (DIY).

Here's a detailed breakdown of the key cost components:

Business Setup and Legal Formalities

- **Business Registration (LLC/Sole Proprietor/Corp.):**

    State Filing Fees: These vary widely by state. You can expect fees to range from $50 to $500+ for a domestic LLC (formed in the state where you operate). For example, California is around $70, while Massachusetts can be $500. Some states also have annual report or franchise tax fees (e.g., California's $800 annual franchise tax, though some states have none).

    Registered Agent Service (Optional but Common): If you don't want to use your home address or need a professional service to receive a legal document, a registered agent service costs $50 - $300 annually.

Doing Business as (DBA) name Registration (if applicable): If you're a sole proprietorship operating under a business name different from your legal name, this fee is typically $10 - $150.

- **Employer Identification Number (EIN):** It is free and needed for taxes and banking. Apply online via IRS.gov.
- **Business Bank Account:** Generally, $0 to open, but check for minimum balance requirements or monthly service fees. Choose a bank that supports international wire transfers.
- **Local/State Business Licenses:** These are highly specific to your city, county and nature of business. A general business license might be $50 - $400. Product-specific permits (e.g., for food, alcohol, or certain regulated goods) can be much higher and specific inspections or certifications.
- **Legal Counsel (Optional but Recommended for Complexities):** While not an upfront mandatory fee for simple setups, consulting an attorney for contract review (especially international sales contracts), intellectual property protection, or complex export compliance can cost $1000 - $5000. Budgeting for occasional consultations as needed is a wise investment as you grow.

Product and Sourcing Costs

- **Initial Inventory Purchase:** Approx. $500 - $3000+ depends on product type and minimum order quantity (MOQ). Start small with scalable products.

- **Samples for Buyers or Testing:** $50 - $500, for quality testing or sending to buyers.
- **Product Packaging and Labeling:** If you opt for branded boxes or specialized protective packaging, cost will increase. This can range from $1 - $10 per unit for custom boxes, plus design fees. Boxes, tape, bubble wrap, labels can be relatively inexpensive, starting from $20 - $100 for initial stock.

Marketing and Sales

- **Website and E-commerce platform:** For Domain name and Hosting (e.g., Squarespace, Wix, Shopify, GoDaddy) $50 - $600 per year, depending on the plan chosen by you. WordPress with Woo commerce can be cheaper hosting, $5 - $30 per month.
- **B2B Marketplace Fees**: Many platforms like Alibaba, ExportHub, Tradekey, Global Sources, IndiaMart offer basic fee listing in the subscription of approx. $500 annually. Their plans change from time to time.
- **Online Advertising (Optional, Scalable):** Set your budget and target international buyers through Google Ads and Social Media Ads (Facebook, Instagram, LinkedIn) using paid campaigns as little as $50 - $200 per month.

Logistics and Freight

- **Freight Forwarding Services:** $200 - $1500 per shipment, based on volume, destination and mode (Air/Sea). Forwarders assist with booking, customs and compliance.
- **Customs Brokerage (If used):** $100 - $400, It is optional for small shipments required for larger or complex exports.

- **Courier/Postage Costs:** $50 - $500 for small packages (USPS, DHL, FedEx)
- **Cargo Insurance (Optional):** $50 - $200 per shipment, it protects against damage/loss.

Export Compliance and Documentation

- **Export License (If required):** Free - $250, Check if needed for restricted goods (BIS, ITAR, EAR). Many goods have no license required.
- **Schedule B Classification:** It is Free, and used for filing export information through AES (Automated Export System).
- **Certificate of Origin:** $25 - $100, may be required by the importing country for customs duties or trade agreement benefits and it is issued by the Chamber of Commerce.
- **Commercial Invoice, Packing List, Bill of Lading:** Free - $200, Templates available or Prepared by a freight forwarder.

Payment Methods

- **Upfront payment (Wire transfer, PayPal, Stripe):** 2.9% - 4.4% per transaction. Ideal for new businesses and small orders to minimize risk.
- **Letter of Credit (LCs):** Provide a high level of security for both parties but involve bank fees and can be complex. More suitable for larger, established details
- **Export Credit Insurance:** Consider this from the Export-Import Bank of the U.S. (EXIM Bank) to protect against non-payment by the foreign buyers. EXIM Bank also offers loan guarantees.

Estimated Minimum Investment

This is a general estimate, as costs can vary significantly by state and product.

1. **Business Registration (LLC):** $50 - $500 annually (state filing fees)
2. **Employer Identification Number (EIN):** $0
3. **Basic Website/Online Presence:** $50 - $600 annually (domain, hosting, simple template; can be less with free tools)
4. **Initial Product Sourcing/Samples:** Highly variable, but could start with $0 (dropshipping/broker) to $500 - $3000+ for small product batches.
5. **Marketing (Initial online ads, networking events):** $50 - $600 per year (leverage free government resources and organic social media first).
6. **Initial Shipping/Documentation (for first few small orders, assumes buyer covers most freight):** $200 - $1500 (per shipment, based on volume, destination and mode (Air/Sea).
7. **Working Capital/Contingency:** $500 - $1000

Total Estimated Minimum Investment: $500 - $3000+ for a very lean, low inventory start-up. This assumes you operate from a home office and leverage free or low cost online tools and government assistance programs.

Key U.S. Resources for Exporters:

- **U.S. Commercial Service (Trade.gov):** Your go-to resource for market research, trade events and direct assistance from trade specialists.

- **Small Business Administration (sba.gov):** Offers counseling, training and financial programs (like the STEP grant and export finance programs).
- **Export-Import Bank of the U.S. (exim.gov) EXIM Bank:** Provides financing and credit insurance to U.S. exporters.
- **U.S. Customs and Border Protection (cbp.gov):** For information on import/export regulations and duties.

U.S. Government Export Loans for Businesses

The U.S. government offers various export loan programs and assistance to businesses, primarily through the Small Business Administration (SBA), the Export-Import Bank of the United States (EXIM Bank) and Foreign Agricultural Services (FAS). These programs are designed to reduce financial risk and provide working capital for exporters. Here's a breakdown of the key options:

SBA Export Loan Programs

Explore SBA financing programs to establish your exporting program and upgrade your export production facilities. There are also programs to enable you to acquire, construct, renovate, modernize, improve or expand facilities and equipment to be used in the United States to produce goods or services involved in international trade.

- **Export Express Program:** Provides small businesses that have export potential with funds to cover the initial costs of entering an export market. The program offers up to

$500,000 in export development financing to buy or produce goods or to provide services for export. The loan proceeds can be used for most business purposes, including expansion, equipment purchases, working capital, inventory or real estate acquisitions.

- **International Trade Loan Program:** Provides U.S. businesses that are preparing to engage in or are already engaged in international trade, or are adversely affected by competition from imports with up to $5 million in financing to upgrade equipment and facilities. Although this loan program can also be used to refinance existing indebtedness that is not structured with reasonable terms and conditions, it cannot be used to purchase a business.
- **Export Working Capital Program:** Provides up to $5 million in short-term, transaction-specific working capital loans to U.S. small business exporters. Uses of this financing include: pre-export financing of labor and materials; and post-shipment financing of the accounts receivable generated from transaction-specific overseas sales.
- **7(a) Export Working Capital Program:** SBA's 7(a) WCP is a pilot loan program offering monitored lines of credit within the 7(a) loan program. The 7(a) WCP can support a range of financing needs for growing small businesses and brings together the best features of the existing permanent 7(a) line of credit delivery methods. Provide SBA 7(a) guaranteed lines of credit up to $5 million.

Recent changes to SBA loan policies

The SBA released a new version of the loan origination standard operating procedures (SOP 50 10 8) that affect various loan programs, including export loans. Key changes include:

Ownership Requirements: SBA loans will be restricted to small businesses with 100% of direct and indirect owners, loan guarantors, and key employees (such as top-level managers) who are U.S. citizens, U.S. nationals, or lawful permanent residents (LPRs). This is a change from the previous long-standing policy in the programs, which allowed assistance to any business 51% or more owned by U.S. citizens, U.S. nationals, and LPRs.

No Credit Elsewhere: The new SOP also tightens the "no credit elsewhere" requirement.

Limited Personal Resources: The new SOP reinstates a limited personal resources test—lenders must check if any owner has liquid resources to substitute for the loan, after providing allowances for savings for retirement, college, and future medical needs.

Collateral: The new SOP will require collateral for almost all loans—the threshold for requiring collateral will be $50,000 (from $500,000).

Equity Injection: Borrowers will be required to contribute an equity injection of 10% of project costs for start-up businesses and changes of ownership.

Business Credit Score: The minimum business credit score will rise from 155 to 165.

EXIM Bank of the U.S.

For many U.S. exporters, a lack of financing can stand in the way of global growth. EXIM has several forms of support that can provide a solution:

- **Working Capital Loan Guarantee:** Provided your business is at least one-year-old; has goods that have at least 50% US content and are manufactured in the US and exported from the US, EXIM can work with your private lender to help secure financing for international sales by providing a guarantee on principal and interest for 90% of export-related Accounts Receivable and 75% of export-related Inventory. A lender receives a loan "guarantee" from EXIM, guaranteeing repayment for a percentage of the loan if the borrower ((i.e., U.S. exporter) defaults. You can use the loan from your bank to pay for the labor, materials, and other inputs required to fulfill sales. EXIM doesn't replace your private bank; it simply backs their loan and increases your borrowing power.
- **Export Credit Insurance:** An insurance policy for your foreign accounts receivable provides protection against the risk of buyer nonpayment. When EXIM backs your foreign receivables, private lenders are often willing to lend against assets otherwise excluded from the borrowing base. The bottom line for your business: same collateral, a larger borrowing base, and a better cash flow.
- **Direct Loan/Buyer Financing:** EXIM's direct loans help U.S. companies secure competitive financing for their international buyers. EXIM provides fixed-rate financing - up to 15 years in general and up to 22 years for renewable energy projects - to creditworthy international buyers in both the private and public sector, and finance local costs up to 50 percent. With EXIM's direct loans, international

buyers get competitive term financing that may previously have been unavailable.

EXIM direct loans to international buyers are generally used for financing purchases of U.S. capital equipment and services. Prior to approving certain transactions, EXIM will consider the economic impact of a particular transaction (see Economic Impact policies) and the environmental effects (see Environment policies).

Here coverage is available for medium-term and long-term transactions. The total level of EXIM support will be less than 85 percent of the value of all eligible goods and services in the U.S. supply contract or 100 percent of the U.S. content in all eligible goods and services in the U.S. supply contract.

U.S. Department of Agriculture (USDA) Export Assistance

The USDA, primarily through its FAS, offers a variety of services and programs that help U.S. agricultural exporters succeed in the global marketplace.

- **Market Access Program (MAP):** Through the MAP, FAS partners with U.S. agricultural trade associations, cooperatives, state regional trade groups and small businesses to share the costs of overseas marketing and promotional activities that help build commercial export markets for U.S. agricultural products and commodities.

  MAP reaches virtually every corner of the globe, helping build markets for a wide variety U.S. farm and food products. FAS provides cost-share assistance to eligible U.S. organizations for activities such as consumer advertising, public relations, point-of-sale demonstrations, participation in trade fairs and exhibits, market research, and technical assistance.

- **Export Credit Guarantee Program (GSM-102):** The GSM-102 program provides credit guarantees to encourage financing of commercial exports of U.S. agricultural products. By reducing financial risk to lenders, credit guarantees encourage exports to buyers in countries — mainly developing countries — that have sufficient financial strength to have foreign exchange available for scheduled payments.

  The program is available to exporters of:

➢ high-value, consumer-oriented, processed products such as frozen foods, fresh produce, meats, condiments, wine and beer;

➢ intermediate products such as hides, flour and paper products; and

➢ bulk products such as grains, oilseeds and rice.

Methods of Payment

To succeed in today's global marketplace and win sales against foreign competitors, exporters must offer their customers attractive sales terms supported by the appropriate payment methods. Because getting paid in full and on time is the ultimate goal for each export sale, an appropriate payment method must be chosen carefully to minimize the payment risk while also accommodating the needs of the buyer.

Key Points

- International trade presents a spectrum of risk, which causes uncertainty over the timing of payments between the exporter (seller) and importer (foreign buyer).
- For exporters, any sale is a gift until payment is received.
- Therefore, exporters want to receive payment as soon as possible, preferably as soon as an order is placed or before the goods are sent to the importer.
- For importers, any payment is a donation until the goods are received.
- Therefore, importers want to receive the goods as soon as possible but to delay payment as long as possible, preferably until after the goods are resold to generate enough income to pay the exporter.

There are five primary methods of payment for international transactions:

1. **Cash-in-Advance**

With cash-in-advance payment terms, an exporter can avoid credit risk because payment is received before the ownership of the goods is transferred. For international sales, wire transfers and credit cards are the most commonly used cash-in-advance options available to exporters. With the advancement of the Internet, escrow services are becoming another cash-in-advance option for small export transactions. However, requiring payment in advance is the least attractive option for the buyer, because it creates unfavorable cash flow. Foreign buyers are also concerned that the goods may not be sent if payment is made in advance. Thus, exporters who insist on this payment method as their sole manner of doing business may lose to competitors who offer more attractive payment terms.

2. Letters of Credit

Letters of credit (LCs) are one of the most secure instruments available to international traders. An LC is a commitment by a bank on behalf of the buyer that payment will be made to the exporter, provided that the terms and conditions stated in the LC have been met, as verified through the presentation of all required documents. The buyer establishes credit and pays his or her bank to render this service. An LC is useful when reliable credit information about a foreign buyer is difficult to obtain, but the exporter is satisfied with the creditworthiness of the buyer's foreign bank. An LC also protects the buyer since no payment obligation arises until the goods have been shipped as promised.

3. Documentary Collections

A documentary collection (D/C) is a transaction whereby the exporter entrusts the collection of the payment for a sale to its bank (remitting bank), which sends the documents that its buyer needs to the importer's bank (collecting bank), with instructions to release the documents to the buyer for payment. Funds are received from the importer and remitted to the exporter through the banks involved in the collection in exchange for those documents. D/Cs involve using a draft that requires the importer to pay the face amount either at sight (document against payment) or on a specified date (document against acceptance). The collection letter gives instructions that specify the documents required for the transfer of title to the goods. Although banks do act as facilitators for their clients, D/Cs offer no verification process and limited recourse in the event of non-payment. D/Cs are generally less expensive than LCs.

4. Open Account

An open account transaction is a sale where the goods are shipped and delivered before payment is due, which in international sales is typically in 30, 60 or 90 days. Obviously, this is one of the most advantageous options to the importer in terms of cash flow and cost, but it is consequently one of the highest risk options for an exporter. Because of intense competition in export markets, foreign buyers often press exporters for open account terms since the extension of credit by the seller to the buyer is more common abroad. Therefore, exporters who are reluctant to extend credit may lose a sale to their competitors. Exporters can offer competitive open account terms while substantially mitigating the risk of non-payment by using one or more of the appropriate trade finance techniques covered later in this Guide. When offering open account terms, the exporter can seek extra protection using export credit insurance.

5. Consignment

Consignment in international trade is a variation of open account in which payment is sent to the exporter only after the goods have been sold by the foreign distributor to the end customer. An international consignment transaction is based on a contractual arrangement in which the foreign distributor receives, manages, and sells the goods for the exporter who retains title to the goods until they are sold. Clearly, exporting on consignment is very risky as the exporter is not guaranteed any payment and its goods are in a foreign country in the hands of an independent distributor or agent. Consignment helps exporters become more competitive on the basis of better availability and faster delivery of goods. Selling on consignment can also help exporters reduce the direct costs of storing and managing inventory. The key to success in exporting on consignment is to partner with a reputable and trustworthy foreign distributor or a third-party logistics provider. Appropriate insurance should be in place to cover consigned goods in transit or in possession of a foreign distributor as well as to mitigate the risk of non-payment.

Managing Currency Exchange Risks

How to Accept Payment in Foreign Currency for Exports?

Foreign exchange (FX) risk exposure is often overlooked by small and medium-sized enterprises (SMEs) that wish to enter, grow, and succeed in global markets. Although most U.S. SME exporters prefer to trade in U.S. dollars, creditworthy foreign buyers today are increasingly requesting that payment be accepted in their local currency. To a U.S. exporter who chooses to trade in foreign currency, FX risk exposure is the potential financial losses due to foreign currency depreciation against the U.S. dollar when payment is due. Obviously, this exposure can be avoided by insisting on trading only in U.S. dollars.

However, such an approach may result in losing export opportunities to competitors who are more flexible in the choice of payment currency by their foreign buyers. Trading only in U.S. dollars could also result in non-payment when foreign buyers find their U.S. dollar-denominated obligations magnified due to local currency depreciation.

While the risk of non-payment can be mitigated by export credit insurance, such "what-if" protection is meaningless if export opportunities are lost due to a "payment in U.S. dollars only" policy. To remain competitive in global markets, U.S. exporters should consider being flexible in accepting payment in foreign currency while exploring ways to proactively manage FX risk exposure.

Characteristics of Foreign Currency-Denominated Export Sales	
Applicability	Recommended for use (a) in competitive global markets, and (b) when foreign buyers insist on paying in their local currency.
Risk	Exporters are exposed to the risk of currency exchange losses unless FX risk management techniques are used.
Pros	Competitive payment terms to win more sales. Reduced non-payment risk resulting from local currency depreciation.
Cons	Cost and burden of managing FX risk. No potential profit from favorable FX movements except when using FX Options hedge.

Key Points

- Most foreign buyers prefer to pay in their local currency to avoid FX risk exposure.
- Exporters who choose to trade in foreign currency could boost their competitiveness and win more sales.
- The volatile nature of the FX market poses a risk to exporters, as unfavorable FX rate movements may cause significant financial losses from otherwise profitable export sales.
- When export sales are denominated in foreign currency, exporters could minimize FX risk exposure by using one or more of the FX risk management techniques.
- The primary objective of FX risk management is not to aim to make a profit, but to minimize potential financial losses resulting from unpredictable and unfavorable FX movements.

FX Risk Management Techniques

Several techniques are available for reducing short-term FX risk exposure, which are suitable for new-to-export SMEs or exporters who are exploring accepting payment in foreign currency. The FX instruments outlined below are available in all major currencies and are offered by numerous commercial banks and FX service providers. However, some techniques may be impractical or cost prohibitive for certain SME exporters.

Cash-in-Advance in Foreign Currency

One way exporters could avoid FX exposure is to demand cash-in-advance payment for foreign currency-denominated sales. The exporters can then immediately calculate the expected net proceeds in home currency using the spot exchange rate, which is the current exchange rate of two currencies.

- **Natural Hedges**

A way to minimize FX risk exposure is to find natural hedges, that is, matching foreign currency receipts with foreign currency expenditures. For example, an American exporter who receives payment in pesos from a Mexican buyer may use pesos for other purposes such as paying agents' commissions or paying another Mexican trading partner for supplies.

If the pesos receipts and payments are comparable in value, FX risk is minimized as the exporter will rarely need to convert pesos into U.S. dollars. The risk is further reduced if those peso-denominated transactions are conducted on a regular basis.

- **FX Forward Hedge**

The most popular way of hedging FX risk is using a forward contract, which enables the exporter to sell a set amount of foreign currency at a predetermined exchange rate at a pre-specified time in the future with a delivery date from three days to one year into the future. For example, a U.S. exporter agrees to accept payment in euros for 1 million euros' worth of goods sold to a German company on a 60-day term.

In fear of the euro depreciating in the next 60 days, the U.S. exporter engages in a forward contract today at the forward exchange rate of one euro to 1.25 U.S. dollars. This forward contract helps the U.S. exporter minimize FX risk exposure by ensuring the conversion of 1 million euros to 1.25 million U.S. dollars, regardless of what happens to the dollar-euro exchange rate in 60 days.

However, if the German buyer fails to pay on time, the U.S. exporter will still be obligated to deliver 1 million euros in 60 days. Hence, when using forward contracts to hedge FX risk, exporters are advised to pick forward delivery dates conservatively or engage in a "window forward contract" which allows for delivery between two dates instead of a specific settlement date.

If the foreign currency is collected sooner, the exporter could hold on to it until the delivery date or could "swap" the old FX contract for one with a new delivery date at a minimal cost. Note that fees or charges for forward contracts are very minimal as the FX trader makes a "spread" by buying at one price and selling to someone else at a higher price.

- **FX Options Hedge**

If an exporter has a large transaction quoted in foreign currency and/or there exists a significant time period between quote and acceptance of the offer, an FX option may be worth considering. For an exporter, using the FX option to hedge currency risk is like buying insurance against foreign currency depreciation.

Under an FX option, the exporter acquires the right, but not the obligation, to exchange the foreign currency into home currency at a specified rate on or before the expiration date of the option.

As opposed to a forward contract, the exporter who purchases an FX option has to pay a premium, which is similar to an insurance premium. If the value of the foreign currency goes down, the exporter is protected from the loss.

On the other hand, if the value of the foreign currency goes up, the exporter simply walks away from the option contract and sells the foreign currency at a more favorable rate in the spot market. While

FX options provide flexibility, they are more costly than FX forward contracts.

Case Studies

A Student Who Started Exporting Part-Time

Here is a hypothetical case study illustrating how a student in the U.S. might start exporting part-time, leveraging available resources.

Name: Jessica Miller

Age: 23

University: University of California, Berkeley

Major: Environmental Science with a minor in Business

Location: San Francisco, California

Initial Capital: $2000

Goal: To build an eco-conscious, export-based skincare brand targeting niche buyers abroad

Business Type: Part-time side hustle while studying

Step 1: Market Research - Identifying a Global Opportunity

Jessica noticed the growing international demand for clean, non-toxic skincare products, especially in:

- Southeast Asia (Singapore, Thailand)
- Middle East (UAE, Saudi Arabia)
- Europe (France, Germany, UK)

She used:

- Google Trends for keyword demand (e.g., "organic face oil", "paraben-free moisturizer")
- Amazon Global to study product categories
- Facebook groups and Reddit threads related to skincare

She identified a niche: organic facial oil and vegan lip balms made from U.S. sourced ingredients.

Step 2: Product Development and Sourcing

Jessica collaborated with a local natural skincare lab in California that offered white-label manufacturing:

- Selected 2 starter products:
    - ➔ Rosehip + Jojoba Face Oil
    - ➔ Vegan Shea Butter Lip Balm
- Requested small batch production (100 units each)
- Cost: ~ $7/unit for oil, $4/unit for balm

She ensured the products were:

- USDA Organic-certified ingredients
- No animal testing
- Complaint with basic FDA cosmetic labeling

Step 3: Business Setup

- Business Structure: Sole Proprietorship under the name "Pure Glow Naturals"
- EIN: Applied online via IRS
- No Export License Required (classified under Schedule B for cosmetics, ECCN not controlled)
- Registered with FDA Voluntary Cosmetic Registration Program (VCRP)

Step 4: Online Presence and Branding

- Built a simple Shopify store with international checkout
- Created a brand identity: clean, minimalist, earth-friendly
- Focused on transparency: full ingredient list, sourcing story

- Uploaded before/after photos and testimonials from friends

Step 5: Marketing and Finding International Buyers

Jessica used a mix of online and personal tactics:

- Joined international skincare communities on Instagram and TikTok
- She partnered with a micro-influencer all over the world
- Listed products on Etsy and eBay with international shipping
- Reached out to eco-friendly boutiques in Germany and South Korea via email

Step 6: Shipping and Fulfillment

She handled order packing herself using eco-friendly packaging.

Shipping Method:

- USPS First Class Package International (for small parcels under 4 lbs)
- Used ShipStation to compare rates and print labels

Shipping Costs:

- ~ $16-$20 to Europe/Asia per order
- Factored into retail price or added at checkout

First Export Sale

After 4 weeks, she received her first order from a customer Singapore:

- 1 Face Oil ($28) + 1 Lip Balm ($12)
- Shipping: ~ $18
- Total received: ~ $58
- Cost of goods + shipping: ~ $30

- Net profit: ~ $28

Step 7: Growing Gradually

- Reinvested profits to expand into travel-size kits
- Gained 2 repeat wholesale customers in Dubai and Germany
- Started applying for grants for women-owned businesses through local small business centers
- Registered for the U.S. Commercial Service webinars to learn about export compliance

Result after 6 Months

Metric	Value
Order/Month	~25-30
Monthly Revenue	~$1900-$2300
Net Profit (Part-Time)	~$700/month
Export Destinations	UAE, Singapore, Germany, Japan, France, Canada
Products Offered	5 (face oil, balm, cleanser, toner, mask)

Key Takeaways

- Start with a small batch to test the market before scaling
- U.S.- made natural skincare is highly valued abroad when marketed with authenticity
- Student entrepreneurs can leverage campus resources, online tools and niche markets
- Keep packaging simple but compliant with both U.S. and foreign cosmetic labeling guidelines

The Challenge: As a full-time student, she has main challenges were:

- Limited Capital: She couldn't afford to buy and hold a large inventory of products
- Logistics and Time: She had no experience with international shipping, customs or managing a high volume of orders on her own
- Risk of Non-Payment: She was concerned about shipping products internationally without getting paid

A Job Professional Who Started Exporting Part-Time

Here is a hypothetical case study about a job professional in the U.S. who started an export business. This scenario is distinct from a student's experience, as a professional has different resources, constraints and expertise.

Name: Daniel Roberts

Age: 36

Location: Chicago, Illinois

Full-Time Job: Work at a Hotel

Export Business: Home improvement tools and accessories

Initial Capital: $3500

Time Commitment: 8-10 hours/week

Export Model: Small-scale B2C and selected B2B orders via online platforms

Step 1: Identifying the Export Opportunity

The U.S.- Made power tools and home improvement hardware are in high demand in China, India, Japan, South Korea, Australia, Germany, the U.K., Brazil and Mexico.

Daniel noticed:

- High demand for durable, U.S.-made brands
- Lack of direct access for small buyers in developing countries
- Untapped niche for refurbished or closeout from liquidation stores

He selected initial products:

- Screwdriver sets
- Cordless drills (refurbished)
- Tool belts and accessories

Step 2: Business Setup

- Structure: Formed an LLC online ("Eagle Trade Tools LLC")
- EIN: Registered through IRS website
- Banking: Opened a business checking account at a local bank
- Seller Account: Created profiles on eBay, Amazon and Alibaba
- Export Licensing: Not required for the tools under EAR99 (he verified using the BIS Decision Tree)

Step 3: Product Sourcing

He sourced products from:

- Local liquidation warehouses
- Home Depot/Lowes clearance sales
- Online auctions (GovDeals, Liquidation.com)

He ensured:

- Products were tested and functional
- Packaging was durable for export

- Product descriptions were accurate and clear

Step 4: Export Logistics and Shipping

- Used UPS and USPS for small parcels
- Partnered with a freight forwarder for consolidated shipments
- Used HTS Schedule B codes to classify his goods for customs
- Labeled and packed items per international standards

Step 5: Finding International Buyers

He focused on:

- Facebook groups and forums for Latin American contractors
- WhatsApp broadcast lists for small hardware retailers
- eBay international listings with global shipping enabled
- Cold emailing small tool stores in Panama and the Dominican Republic

First Export Sale

Within 3 weeks:

- Sold a set of refurbished Dewalt cordless drills to a buyer in the Dominican Republic
- Sale Price: ~ $180
- Shipping Cost: ~ $48
- Net Profit: ~$55 after fees

Step 6: Scaling Up Part-Time

Over the next 6 months, Daniel:

- Created a small Google site with a catalog of available tools

- Joined webinars of International Trade Administration (ITA)
- Registered with the Illinois Small Business Development Center (SBDC)
- Hired a freelance virtual assistant to manage listings and messages

6-Month Results

Metric	Result
Monthly Revenue	~$3500-$4200
Average Profit Margi	25-30%
Export Destinations	Panama, Jamaica, Nigeria, Colombia
Inventory Size	~200 SKUs
Time Spent Weekly	~10 hours (mostly evenings/weekends)

The Challenge:

- Limited Time: As a full-time professional, Daniel's time was a major constraint. He needed a business model that was not overly demanding of his nights and weekends
- Capital and Risk: While he had a steady income, he was unwilling to risk his family's finances on a new venture. He needed a low-capital, low-risk startup model
- Finding Customers: He had no formal international sales network outside of his corporate job
- Compliance: The specialized parts he was dealing with could have complex export control regulations

A Job Seeker Who Turned Unemployment into Opportunity

Here is a hypothetical case study of a job seeker who turned unemployment into an opportunity by starting an export business from the U.S.-with limited capital, no prior experience in international trade and a strong desire to rebuild.

Name: Kevin Thompson

Age: 29

Location: Atlanta, Georgia

Background: Former retail store worker

Initial Capital: $1000 (from saving and unemployment benefits)

Motivation: Wanted to build an independent income source using U.S. products

Export Focus: American-made consumer health and wellness products

Time Available: Full-time at the beginning due to job loss

Step 1: Mindset Shift-From Job Seeker to Exporter

After months of applying for jobs with no luck, Kevin joined a free online webinar hosted by the U.S. Small Business Administration (SBA) titled "How to Start an Export Business".

This introduced him to:

- Global demand for U.S. consumer goods
- Government support for new exporters
- Opportunities even with low capital and no prior trade experience

Step 2: Product Selection-Starting Small, selling what he believed in

Kevin chose a niche he personally used and trusted, natural U.S.-made vitamins and dietary supplements

Examples:

- Melatonin sleep aids
- Omega-3 capsules
- Multivitamins for men/women

These products had:

- High global demand
- Small size-low shipping cost
- Easy online sourcing from Costco, Walmart and wholesale platforms

Step 3: Setting Up the Business

- Business Name: Global Essentials Export
- Entity: Registered as a sole proprietorship
- EIN: Obtained online from the IRS
- Banking: Opened a business account with a credit union
- Export License: Not required (he verified under EAR for OTC supplements)
- Customs Code: Found Schedule B Code Under HS 210690 (food supplements)

Step 4: Selling Online-Low risk entry strategy

He created seller profile on:

- eBay with global shipping turned on
- Facebook Marketplace (International groups)
- WhatsApp groups used by West African and Caribbean buyers
- Added a Shopify store

He posted:

- Clear photos of U.S.-made supplement bottles
- Short descriptions with dosage and benefits
- Trust-building information like "100% U.S. Authentic", expiry date and source location

First Export Order

Kevin received his first international order within 2 weeks:

- 1 bottle of Vitamin D3 to a buyer in Trinidad & Tobago
- Cost: $9
- Sold for: $22
- Shipping: $6 (via USPS first-class international)
- Net profit: ~$7

Step 5: Scaling Gradually

With repeat orders, Kevin reinvested his profits:

- Added items like protein bars, joint health capsules
- Partnered with a Caribbean-based mini-mart for small bulk orders
- Used PayPal and Wise for receiving international payments
- Learned how to use ShipStation for managing logistics efficiently

Step 6: Support and Learning

He leaned on public resources:

- SBA free mentoring (SCORE)
- Export-U online training
- U.S. Commercial Services newsletters for market updates
- Joined Facebook groups for small exporters and learned from peer advice

After 6 Months

Metric	Result
Monthly Revenue	~$2500
Profit Margin	30-35%
Countries Exported to	Jamaica, Nigeria, Bahamas, UAE
Product Types	~30 SKUs
Business Hours	~25 hrs./week

The Challenge:

- Limited Capital: With only ~$1000 in savings, he couldn't afford bulk inventory, ads or a fancy website
- Lack of Expert Knowledge: He had no prior knowledge of international trade, customs or documentation
- Trust with buyers: Buyers abroad were skeptical about buying from a new, unknown seller
- Shipping Costs and Delays: International shipping was expensive and sometimes slow

References

https://www.trade.gov/why-export

https://exportpotential.intracen.org/en/products/tree-map?fromMarker=i&exporter=842&toMarker=w&market=w&whatMarker=k

https://beta.trade.gov/article?id=Preparing-your-Product-for-Export-Product-Adaption

https://www.trade.gov/conducting-market-research

https://www.trade.gov/selecting-international-markets

https://www.trade.gov/free-trade-agreement-overview

https://www.trade.gov/industry-classification-systems

https://beta.trade.gov/article?id=Trade-Missions

https://beta.trade.gov/article?id=US-Department-of-Commerce-Trade-Event-Programs

https://beta.trade.gov/article?id=Foreign-Agricultural-Service

https://beta.trade.gov/article?id=International-Company-Profiles

https://beta.trade.gov/article?id=International-Partner-Search

https://beta.trade.gov/article?id=Finding-Buyers-Program-Customized-Market-Research

https://business.thomasnet.com/about

https://www.foreign-trade.com/about.htm

https://www.wholesalecentral.com/aboutus.htm

https://www.trade.gov/

https://www.fas.usda.gov/about-fas

https://www.exportportal.com/about

https://globaltradehelpdesk.org/en/about/the-initiative

References

https://www.tradekey.com/about-us/

https://www.exporthub.com/ot/about-us

https://www.globalsources.com/corporate/en/about/

https://www.indiamart.com/

https://in.solutions.kompass.com/

https://www.sba.gov/business-guide/launch-your-business/choose-business-structure

https://www.sba.gov/business-guide/launch-your-business/choose-your-business-name

https://www.sba.gov/business-guide/launch-your-business/register-your-business

https://stripe.com/in/resources/more/how-to-file-for-an-ein-a-quick-guide-for-businesses#preparing-to-file-for-an-ein

https://deliberatedirections.com/how-to-register-your-business-with-the-irs-and-obtain-an-ein/

https://www.maersk.com/logistics-explained/customs-and-compliance/2023/09/27/us-import-export-license-what-it-is-and-how-to-get-it

https://envoy.com/workplace-compliance-security-safety/export-administration-regulations-compliance

https://www.shippingsolutions.com/blog/whats-the-difference-between-a-schedule-b-code-and-an-hs-number

https://www.census.gov/foreign-trade/schedules/b/index.html

https://beta.trade.gov/article?id=Determine-your-HS-or-Schedule-B-number

https://www.cbp.gov/trade/aes/introduction

https://www.census.gov/foreign-trade/aes/ace-aesdirect.html

https://www.trade.gov/filing-your-export-shipments-through-automated-export-system-aes

https://www.census.gov/foreign-trade/aes/aesdirect/register_access_aesdirect.pdf

https://www.trade.gov/common-export-documents

https://www.trade.gov/filing-your-export-shipments-through-automated-export-system-aes

https://grow.exim.gov/blog/shippers-letter-of-instruction-0

https://grow.exim.gov/blog/incoterms2020

https://legacy.export.gov/article?id=Incoterms-Overview

https://www.trade.gov/customs-brokers-and-freight-forwarders

https://legacy.export.gov/article?id=Packing

https://legacy.export.gov/article?id=Labeling

https://legacy.export.gov/article?id=Branding-Labeling-and-Packaging

https://www.privacyshield.gov/ps/article?id=Cargo-Insurance

https://www.trade.gov/business-development-financing

https://www.trade.gov/export-working-capital

https://www.sba.gov/partners/lenders/7a-loan-program/7a-working-capital-pilot-program

https://www.congress.gov/crs-product/IN12549#:~:text=The%20SBA%20released%20a%20new,effective%20on%20June%201%2C%202025.

https://www.exim.gov/solutions/get-financing

https://www.exim.gov/solutions/direct-loan

https://www.fas.usda.gov/programs/market-access-program-map

https://www.trade.gov/methods-payment

References

https://www.trade.gov/report/trade-finance-guide

9 789334 384277

Printed at Repro India Ltd.